MYSTERIES
OF THE
ANOINTING

MYSTERIES
OF THE
ANOINTING

BENNY HINN

CHARISMA
HOUSE

Most Charisma Media products are available at special quantity discounts for bulk purchase for sales promotions, premiums, fundraising, and educational needs. For details, call us at (407) 333-0600 or visit our website at www.charismamedia.com.

MYSTERIES OF THE ANOINTING by Benny Hinn
Published by Charisma House, an imprint of Charisma Media
600 Rinehart Road, Lake Mary, Florida 32746

Unless otherwise noted, Scripture quotations are taken from the King James Version of the Bible.

Scripture quotations marked NIV are taken from the Holy Bible, New International Version®, NIV®. Copyright © 1973, 1978, 1984, 2011 by Biblica, Inc.® Used by permission of Zondervan. All rights reserved worldwide. www.zondervan.com. The "NIV" and "New International Version" are trademarks registered in the United States Patent and Trademark Office by Biblica, Inc.®

Scripture quotations marked NKJV are taken from the New King James Version®. Copyright © 1982 by Thomas Nelson. Used by permission. All rights reserved.

Scripture quotations marked NLT are from the Holy Bible, New Living Translation, copyright © 1996, 2004, 2007. Used by permission of Tyndale House Publishers, Inc., Wheaton, IL 60189. All rights reserved.

All italics in Scripture quotations reflect the author's emphasis.

Visit the author's website at bennyhinn.org.

Cataloging-in-Publication Data is on file with the Library of Congress.

International Standard Book Number: 978-1-63641-067-8
E-book ISBN: 978-1-63641-068-5

22 23 24 25 26 — 9 8 7 6 5 4 3 2 1
Printed in the United States of America

International Standard Book Number 978-1-63641-067-8

e-book ISBN ...

While the author has made every effort to provide accurate internet addresses at the time of publication, neither the publisher nor the author assumes any responsibility for errors or for changes that occur after publication. Further, the publisher has no control over and does not assume any responsibility for author or third-party websites or their content.

CONTENTS

PART III: ANOINTED TO PROPHESY

PART I

ANOINTED FOR LIVING

WELCOME TO *MYSTERIES* OF THE ANOINTING

THE ANOINTING OF the Holy Spirit is desperately needed and necessary today. Its power can be imitated but never duplicated. We must have the anointing's irreplaceable presence, which no other religious effort or spiritual quest can match. This vital equipping of the believer's life is often misunderstood and historically undertaught. The purpose of this book is to reveal mysteries of the anointing that will release the power of God to move in your life in a tangible way.

Scripture sanctions the believer in Jesus as both king and priest before God. We are given the unction to rise to the place of the high calling and to be everything He has promised us we can be. The anointing initiates and confirms our position in Christ Jesus.

Charles Spurgeon, in *The Treasury of David*, an exposition on Psalm 23, wrote: "Every Christian is a priest, but he cannot execute the priestly office without unction, and hence we must go day by day to God the Holy Ghost, that we may have our heads anointed with oil. A priest without oil misses the chief qualification for his office, and the Christian priest lacks his chief fitness for service when he is devoid of new grace."[1]

In recent decades we have seen the emergence of seeker-sensitive churches and ministries that have almost been ashamed of the anointing of the Holy Spirit and the gifts God brings. The anointing has been hidden and covered, and a shallow and powerless generation of believers has replaced those filled with Holy Ghost power. God is going to rescue this generation and restore His church in great power.

This book contains the antidote to the virus that has weakened the body of Christ. The anointing of God is what is required to release the huddled masses of a bound and oppressed generation. Get ready for God to ignite you with fire. The anointing of God fuels the fire of the Holy Spirit. Open your heart to a deeper level of God's mighty anointing, and get ready to burn with fresh passion for God and His purpose for your life.

After nearly four decades of powerful ministry I went through the most painful season of my life. Ministers and believers are not exempt from mental, physical, or emotional pain. God never promised we would not go through hard times. He did promise we would not go through them alone. God has given us the guarantee of His Word that He will never leave us or forsake us.

This time in my life was an excruciatingly painful experience for my family. God sometimes needs to take us off the mountaintop and put us in the valley for us to learn. The valley we walked through lasted three long years. My wife, Suzanne, suffered a personal crisis that reached back decades into her own life. God saw her and our family through it all. Suzanne has shared this personal victory, and many have been encouraged and strengthened by her story.

Through this painful season I learned there are differences in the way God uses His anointing in our lives. There are different anointings that flow through God's people. I didn't realize it until I went through this extremely difficult time in my life. I did not discover this in any school. Only the Holy Spirit could have revealed these things. I saw I could minister under the anointing and the anointing upon my office was not affected at all, yet at home my personal life was struggling.

As a result, I began to ask questions. I wondered how the struggle in my personal life and even the struggle in my spiritual life did not affect the anointing to minister in our live services. Then, to my amazement, I learned the anointing upon my ministry office has nothing to do with the anointing in my life. The anointing in my life is separate.

I began to search the Scriptures. The Lord said, "Out of your innermost being shall flow rivers." He did not say one river. He did not say two or three rivers. God said rivers. He never told us how many rivers. I am still discovering the rivers. It was necessary for me to go through this painful season of my life to realize there are many rivers to the anointing. The Lord later restored my personal life spiritually, emotionally, and physically, but that period was a learning experience. I'm glad there are no wasted years. God can use the pain in our lives for our growth. God does not waste our pain.

Romans 8:28 promises, "And we know that all things work together for good to them that love God, to them who are the called according to his purpose."

I can tell you this: had I not gone through this painful season, I would not be writing this book. I am writing this book because as I have shared this message worldwide, I have discovered this is not a widely known revelation. I have found this illumination of the Holy Spirit regarding the many rivers of the anointing is a fresh concept for God's people. It is revelatory for me, and I have never read about it in a book or heard it taught before.

Let us now dive into the deep and discover the rivers of God's precious anointing.

Chapter 2

UNDERSTANDING MYSTERIES
OF THE ANOINTING

YOU ARE A spirit.
Let that sink in for just a moment. You are not a soul. You are not a body. You are a spirit. You have a soul. You live in a body. But you are a spirit. That's who you are. Your body is not the real you. The real you is your spirit.

At the moment of your salvation, something dynamic happened. The person of the Holy Spirit became one with your spirit. The Scripture is clear on this in 1 Corinthians 6:17, where it says, "He that is joined unto the Lord is one spirit." When the Holy Spirit and your spirit became one, at that moment, life, rebirth, cleansing, renewal, and regeneration took place. The moment this oneness between the Holy Spirit and your spirit took place, a mighty force was released. This force within us is what we call the anointing.

The anointing of God is a vast subject. The study of it is almost endless because it has so many different streams; one book cannot contain it all. Throughout these pages I will discuss some intriguing, hidden matters in the Bible. I call them mysteries of the anointing. I explore why certain things happened the way they did in the lives of the Lord Jesus, Moses, David, and

Paul. Perhaps you've wondered about some of the things that took place in their lives. They are mysteries. But there's an answer to every mystery in the Bible.

As you make your way through the three sections of the book, you'll notice a progression. In exploring the components of the anointing, we see that there are levels that go deeper and deeper. As we advance, you will notice that in the deeper levels, there are fewer who operate in each of these anointing levels.

We start with the inner anointing that everyone receives at salvation, and then we progress to the outer anointing. It is reserved for those God trusts with it, ones who have chosen to dedicate their lives to becoming vessels of God devoted to His ministry. We will also explore the coming Elijah anointing for nations, which very few have ever had.

Most people don't know the anointing exists or, if they do, why it exists. It's an enigma. My goal is to help you navigate through this challenging subject by sharing the Word of God and the experiences I've had in more than forty years of ministry. John 8:32 tells us, "Ye shall know the truth, and the truth shall make you free." The only truth that will set you free is the truth that you know. As you walk through these pages, your understanding of the anointing will grow so that you will become more proficient in moving in your anointing, an instrument of God, finely tuned to His measures.

I've also had the privilege of being close to some of the most remarkable people that ever lived, and I've seen firsthand how God used them. I learned a great deal from working with the Kathryn Kuhlman Foundation for four years and also through my close personal friendships with Rex Humbard and Oral Roberts. I've probably talked with Oral Roberts more than any other human being about the mysteries in this book. In his later years I'd go to his home almost every week, and we'd spend hours and hours together.

You can't be close to people such as these and not learn something. You can't be in your own ministry for decades and not learn something either. Their imprint is certainly on these pages as it is on every aspect of my ministry. Even with their fellowship and teaching, however, after decades of worldwide ministry I didn't understand much of what I am about to share. It wasn't until a few years ago that the Lord gave me many of these profound insights about the anointing. I didn't find them in any book or teaching. I found them by seeking the Lord and His Word. What the Lord revealed to me after I went in search of answers, I share with you now.

THREE MAJOR ANOINTINGS

In the Bible we find three major anointings: the abiding anointing, the empowering anointing, and the dominion anointing.

1. The abiding anointing *H·S·*

> The anointing which ye have received of him abideth in you, and ye need not that any man teach you: but as the same anointing teacheth you of all things, and is truth, and is no lie, and even as it hath taught you, ye shall abide in him.
> —1 JOHN 2:27

The anointing mentioned in 1 John 2:27 is what I call the abiding anointing. This anointing is for living. It's an inner anointing, working from within you to deepen your fellowship with God. As we begin our journey, I want you to notice something that many people miss. The abiding anointing is the anointing for *living*, not doing. This inner anointing affects the

9

spirit of a person. The emphasis of the abiding anointing is not meant for the soul or the body.

The abiding anointing stays in you; it dwells within the child of God. It affects your heart, your life, your walk with God, and your fellowship with Him. It provides the grace to continue in the things of God. Today, know and be aware that the abiding anointing is within you to teach you and help establish you daily. You are not isolated or alone. You are equipped with a continual flow of God's abiding anointing.

2. The empowering anointing

> But ye shall receive power, after that the Holy Ghost is come upon you: and ye shall be witnesses unto me both in Jerusalem, and in all Judaea, and in Samaria, and unto the uttermost part of the earth.
>
> —ACTS 1:8

The anointing that we see in Acts 1:8 is an outer anointing. This empowering anointing affects your ministry and the gifts of the Spirit on your life. This is the anointing for service. It provides the ability to share the gospel with others, whether or not there is a call to a ministry office upon your life.

I'll cover this anointing more thoroughly in two sections: one for all Christians used by God in ministry to others and one for those called to an office or a life-calling ministry position.

The abiding anointing is for everyday living and is available to every believer. The empowering anointing is distinctly for service and therefore applies to those who have dedicated themselves to serving God in ministry to others. It affects the body and soul but not the spirit. It is for *doing*. It does not necessarily affect a person's Christian life or spiritual walk. It is a gift. This outer anointing is given to those who prove themselves faithful to the Lord. Not every Christian chooses to serve, and so not every Christian receives the empowering anointing. I'll discuss that more in a later chapter.

3. The dominion anointing

> It shall come to pass in that day, that his burden shall be taken away from off thy shoulder, and his yoke from off thy neck, and the yoke shall be destroyed because of the anointing.
>
> —ISAIAH 10:27

The dominion anointing of Isaiah 10:27 is a very rare and powerful anointing. This world-changing anointing specifically affects nations; it has the power to build kingdoms or destroy them. Very few have this anointing, which I also call the Elijah anointing. This anointing rested on Moses, Joshua, Isaiah, Jeremiah, Ezekiel, Elijah, Elisha, and a few others in the Old Covenant. It rested on individuals God used prophetically to raise up kingdoms or destroy them.

I believe we are coming into what I call the Elijah realm of the anointing. The Elijah realm is a realm we have rarely seen on earth. Glimpses and seasons of the Elijah realm of the anointing have come and gone. We're coming into the Elijah days again very soon. This anointing is the only anointing that will destroy the spirit of Jezebel, which is the spirit of witchcraft. This anointing cannot be adequately explained in just a few words. I will devote a more complete teaching to this at a later time.

As you progress through this book, you'll see that the responsibilities for each anointing get higher and so do the rewards in the kingdom.

The anointing is the foundation for everything God gives you in life. It took me a long time to learn what I must do to build a solid foundation in my life for God to use me and continue using me, and I'm sharing those insights in this book. They will save you from collapse. These insights will strengthen you to keep you in fellowship with our wonderful Lord Jesus so that you do not fall away.

Chapter 3

THE MYSTERY OF THE ABIDING ANOINTING

T HE ABIDING ANOINTING described in 1 John 2:27 is a vital key for this whole book, so please read that verse now. Underline it here and in your Bible. It reveals a powerful truth that is the foundation for everything else God gives you.

> But the anointing which ye have received of him abideth in you, and ye need not that any man teach you: but as the same anointing teacheth you of all things, and is truth, and is no lie, and even as it hath taught you, ye shall abide in him.
>
> —1 JOHN 2:27

Let's break this verse down to understand what it is saying about this level of anointing, the one that allows you to abide in Jesus because He abides in you. It begins with, "But the anointing which ye have received of him." The first thing I want you to notice is the word *of.* John says this anointing is *of* God, not *from* God.

This anointing *of* Him is separate from the one *from* Him. The one *of* Him is the inner anointing for living described here in 1 John. The one *from* Him is the outer anointing for ministry described in Acts 1:8. There is a reason these words are not the same. It seems simple, but it took me years to discover this, and when you grasp this, it will change your entire understanding. That's why I'm sharing it with you in this book. The anointing for living is *of* God; the anointing for ministry is *from* God.

The phrase *of Him* means that He is the source. This anointing *is* Him; it is not a gift *from* Him. Let me show you what I mean. If I say to someone, "Take this *from* me," it means I have it. If I have it, someone gave it to me. If I have it, it had a beginning. If I have it, it will have an end.

But if I say to someone, "Take this *of* me," they cannot do it because I *am* it. The abiding anointing is *of* Him because it *is* Him. It is the anointing that *He is*. In the Old Testament the Lord said, "I am," which means God doesn't *have* life; God *is* life. God doesn't *have* power; God *is* power. There is a power that He gives as a gift, of course. I'll write about that later. But here I'm talking about who God *is*.

Next, this verse tells us this anointing "abideth in you." This anointing abides. It doesn't come and go. The empowering anointing *from* Him in Acts 1:8 does not abide. God anoints you as you minister, and when you are done ministering, it lifts. The empowering anointing is from the Lord for a certain moment, a specific assignment. It is for a season and a reason. By contrast, the abiding anointing does not leave; it stays. It abides and thickens; it abides and grows; it abides and brings forth the revelation of all things. It *abides*.

Please notice that the Bible says the abiding anointing is *in* you. The empowering anointing (which is the anointing for ministry) rests *on* you. The empowering anointing for ministry comes later, but the abiding anointing comes at salvation.

The Scripture continues, "And ye need not that any man teach you: but as the same anointing teacheth you of all things." The abiding anointing that comes into your spirit and becomes one with your heart at salvation is a revelation anointing. It reveals everything about God. It is endless because it teaches you *all things*.

Why would John say you don't need anyone to teach you? You've got to look at the whole chapter to see that it is a warning to believers. I encourage you to read all of 1 John 2, but for the sake of space, right now we will focus on what John says in verse 26:

> These things have I written unto you concerning them that seduce you.

John was warning that people will try to pull you away from the truth of who Jesus is. *That is the reason he says the anointing abides in you and you don't need anyone to teach you anything.* The abiding anointing teaches you that Jesus, the Son of God, is exactly who He says He is. The Holy Spirit reveals who Jesus is to our hearts. It is the truth, and there is no lie in it.

The minute you are saved, the Holy Spirit becomes one with your spirit. One of the first things that happen is faith explodes in you. By the Holy Spirit you immediately know who the Lord Jesus is in your life. You don't need anyone to teach you who He is. That's why nobody can seduce you. Even though they may try, they cannot succeed because you already have the truth inside you. Jesus is the truth inside you.

CONTRASTING THE ABIDING AND EMPOWERING ANOINTINGS

When John says this abiding anointing "is truth, and is no lie," he means there is no lie in it. It is for revelation and protection. It protects you from deception. It is possible to be deceived with the anointing *on* you but not with the anointing *in* you. Put another way, the outer (empowering) anointing allows deception; the inner (abiding) anointing protects you from deception.

So someone can minister and preach the gospel as the anointing comes *on* him, yet the devil can deceive him. It is possible to be used by the Lord and no longer know the Lord. Think about that for a minute. The Bible says many will come in that day saying, "Lord, Lord, have we not prophesied in thy name? And in thy name have cast out devils? And in thy name done many wonderful works?" and He will say, "I never knew you" (Matt. 7:22–23). It is a staggering truth that a person can know and preach the Bible and be under an anointing for ministry yet not know the Lord. In other words, that person has no fellowship with the Lord, no intimate knowledge of the Lord.

King Saul is a perfect example. He knew how to be king, but he did not know the Lord. David knew the Lord. That's the difference. Knowing the Lord is the key. Knowing Him is the foundation for life and ministry. The greatest revelation of life is having an intimate knowledge of the Lord in a way that He is real to you and manifests Himself in you.

Paul talks about the abiding anointing when he says,

> Now unto him that is able to do exceeding abundantly above all that we ask or think, according to the power that worketh in us.
>
> —EPHESIANS 3:20

Notice he says that it works *in* us, not *through* us. Ephesians 3:20 and 1 John 2:27 are talking about the same anointing: the inner (abiding) anointing for Christian living.

The abiding anointing works in us; the empowering anointing works through us.

The abiding anointing is for walking; the empowering anointing is for working.

The abiding anointing is for revelation and manifestation; the empowering anointing is for demonstration.

With the abiding anointing the Lord manifests Himself in my spirit. He doesn't manifest within me so *others* will know Him; He manifests Himself within me that *I* might know Him. The empowering anointing is for demonstration that others might know Him.

The truth of the abiding anointing in 1 John is for revelation. God is revealing Himself to us. It is also for transformation. It transforms us as Christians, as servants of God, as individuals.

Finally, 1 John 2:27 says, "And even as it hath taught you, ye shall abide in him." This means it will keep you abiding in the Lord. The abiding anointing is so powerful that it ignites the enduring power of God to keep you. Thus, we are kept by the inner anointing.

THREE SIGNS OF THE ABIDING ANOINTING

There are three signs of the abiding anointing: hunger, faith, and love. These three things happen at salvation, the moment you become one with the Lord Jesus. Allow me to explain.

1. Hunger

When a baby is born, he is hungry for food. In the physical realm, hunger is the sign of life. It's the same in the spiritual realm. The minute you were born again, you became one with Jesus and you developed a spiritual hunger. From that moment, spiritual hunger is part of your life. You start seeking more and more of the presence of God through His Word.

2. Faith

The second thing that happens at salvation is an explosion of faith. You know that Jesus is the Son of God, that He died for your sins, and that He rose from the dead. How do you know that reality? You don't need to read it in a book. You know it by the Spirit. The Holy Spirit gives you an inner knowing that you belong to Him, that He loves you, that heaven is your home, that there is power in the blood to set you free, and that you are redeemed. That inner knowing is faith. You receive God-given faith, and therefore, you don't have to convince yourself it's real. The Lord becomes real to you—more real than your own life.

Before I move on, let me quickly explain that there are different types of faith. First is the measure, or seed, of faith. God puts a measure of faith in your life at salvation, and immediately you know He's your God. This is the faith I've been talking about where you know the Lord Jesus is the Savior of your soul.

Next is the fruit of faith. After God has sown the seed of faith in your life, it takes hold of your heart. It grows and bears fruit in your life called the fruit of the Spirit.

Last is the gift of faith. This type of faith is different because it is not for your relationship with God. Instead, the gift of faith is for ministry to others. Every gift for ministry comes under the empowering anointing of Acts 1:8, which I will talk about in a later chapter.

3. Love

The third thing that comes alive at salvation is the Holy Spirit gives you a love for the Lord Jesus you have never known and a desire to know the Lord, a desire to walk with Him, a desire to serve Him. That is love. The minute that oneness with the Lord Jesus takes place, there is a great desire to know Him. The Bible says that even though we haven't seen the Lord Jesus, we love Him (1 Pet. 1:8).

When I got saved, on February 14, 1972, I fell in love with Jesus in a split second. A group of kids in my Toronto high school had been talking to me about Jesus, and I thought they were all crazy. It seemed that all they did was go around saying, "Jesus loves you," and I didn't know how to respond to that. But they would not give up. All through my senior year, they kept telling me Jesus loved me.

On the night of February 13, 1972, something incredible happened. I had a dream that I will never forget. I saw myself on a long stairway going down into a pit. I was chained to other prisoners, and little half-human, half-animal creatures prodded us to keep walking down the stairs. There was no way out, and the stairway kept going deeper and deeper into darkness.

Suddenly an angel appeared right beside me. No one saw him but me, and he motioned for me to come to him. At that moment, my chains fell off. He took me by the hand, and a door opened out of nowhere. The angel still held me by the hand as he led me through the door, took me through the air, and landed me on a street corner right outside one of the windows of my high school building. As soon as we landed in my dream, I woke up. I had no idea what it all meant. I had no idea that the spot where my dream ended would become significant in just a few short hours.

Since I had awoken early, I headed to school and made my way to the library. The group of students who always talked about Jesus invited me to its morning prayer meeting, which was in the library. I thought, "What can it hurt? And maybe it will finally get them off my back." I went to the meeting, and the next thing I knew, the kids were all praying in tongues. I had never heard anyone pray like that before.

I was scared, but at the same time, I felt a presence come over me. It was overwhelming. I didn't know how to say to Jesus, "Come into my heart." None of the kids said, "Here's how you get saved. Pray these words after me." They just kept praying in tongues, and I began crying. It was such an emotional moment.

I put my head down and said out loud, "Jesus, come back!" I said that because I had had a visitation from the Lord when I was eleven, but nothing had happened since then. I knew this was the same Jesus I had encountered at age eleven, so all I could think to say was, "Come back!" The prayer meeting ended shortly after that, and no one said anything to me.

I didn't know what else to do except head to my first class. I knew something had happened to me, but I didn't even know how to describe it. I walked into the classroom late, and the teacher had already begun her lesson. All I could think was, "Jesus is coming back!" Something just told me this inside, and it was all I could think about. I couldn't listen to the lesson, so I just put my head down on my desk. As soon as I put my head down, I could see Jesus in a white robe, walking on the Sea of Galilee, coming toward me. I opened my eyes, and I could still see Jesus.

I began crying so hard right there in class. I cried out, "Jesus, I love You!" The whole class stopped. The teacher didn't know what to do. My cousin sitting next to me kept saying, "Shh! Be quiet!" But I didn't care. I just kept saying, "Jesus, I love You!" because I saw Him coming to me.

All day I kept weeping, and the only thing I could say was, "Jesus, I love You!" Then, as I left school and headed toward the corner of the building, I noticed the library window. Suddenly, my dream from the night before came flooding back. That was the corner where I landed in my dream, and the window in my dream was the window of the library where I had just encountered the Lord Jesus.

Instantly, I knew the Lord was drawing me to Him, and I knew that I loved Him with all my heart. Who put this love in me? It was the Holy Spirit.

The kids who had invited me to the prayer meeting also invited me to church. That Thursday night, I went with them to the Toronto Catacombs, led by Merv Watson and his wife, Merla, who wrote "Jehovah Jireh." The guest speaker that night was

Loren Cunningham, founder of Youth With a Mission (YWAM). At the end of his message, Loren gave an altar call, and I heard the audible voice of the Lord telling me to go down to the altar. That's where I made my public declaration of faith.

HUNGER LEADS TO FELLOWSHIP

The abiding anointing begins to manifest immediately as a hunger for God. When I got saved, I wanted more of what I had tasted of Him when I was eleven. That was hunger. Then, suddenly, I knew I was a child of God. When I got saved, no man told me. I just knew it. The Holy Spirit put that faith in me with such reality. And third, my reaction was, "Jesus, I love You!" Those three things are the signs of life in Jesus, which begin our fellowship with Him: hunger, faith, and love.

The minute your relationship with God begins, hunger leads you to fellowship. Please don't miss that: hunger leads to fellowship. It's simple but profound. The minute we become one with Christ Jesus, the abiding anointing is released, and our fellowship with Him begins.

The minute that intimacy starts, it quickens or ignites the Word. The Bible comes alive. Your relationship with God's Word starts as a result. Hunger for the Lord produces hunger for His Word, not the other way around. When people don't experience hunger for the Lord *before* they hunger for His Word, they become religious. They become worshippers of doctrine, not worshippers of God. They are hungry for knowledge, not for the Lord.

There are Christians today who don't even know the Lord. They know His Word, but they don't know Him. They know what He said, but they don't know the One who said it. There's a lot of knowledge, but there is no anointing, no presence of God evident in their lives. Sadly, these people end up worshipping doctrine instead of worshipping the Lord. And when they worship doctrine, they become legalistic.

I'm sure you know people like this. They know the Bible and will use it against you, but there is no compassion. They don't know how to show the Lord's love. Many of them can teach or preach circles around the rest of us, but they don't know the Lord.

That's what Jesus dealt with when He was on earth. The Pharisees knew the Scriptures, but they had no love or compassion.

Before the apostle Paul's conversion, he knew the Scriptures so well that he killed believers and used the Scriptures to defend his actions. He was blinded by doctrine. That's what it does; it blinds you. But the minute he met the Lord Jesus, it changed everything. Before his conversion, he was a perfect example of a man who knew the Word but not the Lord. He even used the Old Testament Law against the Lord and His people.

It is the same as the Pharisees who came to the Lord and said, "Here's a woman caught in the very act of adultery. The Word says she must be killed. What do You say about it?" What did Jesus say? "He who is without sin, find a rock and throw it." They all walked away. (See John 8:3–11.)

This account demonstrates why you must develop your relationship with the Lord before developing your relationship with His Word. Otherwise there's no balance. Fellowship with God is the foundation of life and ministry. Then, on top of that, you develop your relationship with His Word. Your hunger for Him leads you to know His Word, not the other way around.

When I know Him, I want to know His mind, not the other way around. Knowing Him drives me to know His mind—What does He think about this and that? Then, when I read the Bible, I am not reading law and rules and regulations; I am developing my relationship with the Lord.

Your hunger opens the way into God's presence and causes

God to quicken you, to bring you to life spiritually. The hungrier you are, the more quickened you are by the Spirit. The Bible says, "Taste and see that the LORD is good" (Ps. 34:8). What does that mean? It means when you are hungry, God gives you a taste of His presence and you become hungrier for Him.

As your hunger leads to fellowship, a brand-new chapter opens where not only do you want to know Him, but you want to know the way He thinks. How does He see life? How does He see you? That's where His Word comes in. You cannot know the thoughts of a person until you know the person. When you know the person, then you know his or her ways.

David began to know the Lord before he ever knew His ways. In 2 Samuel 6, when David was on the way to bringing back the ark of the covenant, Uzzah touched it and died. Verses 9 and 10 say David was afraid to bring the ark to his home. He realized, "I need to know the ways of the Lord better." He discovered the Lord's ways through His Word. He was still finding the ways of the Lord.

And then there is Moses. He knew the Lord, but he still said, "Show me Your glory." Moses was saying, "Lord, I want to know You. I want to know Your presence." He was hungry for more. Moses wanted to know the way God thinks, the way He looks at His people. What was he crying for? He wanted to know the glory of the Lord.

God already knew Moses, and Moses knew the Lord. But because of Moses' request, in Exodus 34 God passed before him. Moses wanted to see God's face, but what revealed the Lord to Moses was His attributes, His ways, and His nature.

> And the LORD passed by before him, and proclaimed, The LORD, The LORD God, merciful and gracious, longsuffering, and abundant in goodness and truth, keeping mercy for thousands, forgiving iniquity and transgression and sin, and

that will by no means clear the guilty; visiting the iniquity of the fathers upon the children, and upon the children's children, unto the third and to the fourth generation.

—EXODUS 34:6–7

God revealed Himself through His Word. Psalm 103:7 powerfully confirms this. It says, "He made known his ways unto Moses, his acts unto the children of Israel." When did God do that? In Exodus 33–34 when Moses began crying out.

God revealed His nature, His attributes, to Moses, and Moses perceived all of it in his spirit man. The Bible declares in Hebrews 11 that he saw the sufferings of the Messiah and rejected the pleasures of Egypt. God revealed His ways to him in Exodus 34.

We must understand that the abiding anointing reveals who the Lord is in our lives. The abiding anointing protects our hearts from deception. The abiding anointing causes us to continue in fellowship with the Lord. This anointing resides in us. It is the anointing I have been writing about that produces hunger, faith, and love.

In the next chapter I will examine what it means to practice the presence of God, which is dwelling in the spirit realm, where God's promises are activated. When you experience that depth of communion with the Lord, your presence becomes His presence. Your vessel becomes His vessel. Your eyes become His eyes. Your touch becomes His touch. Your voice becomes His voice. And with that the world will know He's alive!

Chapter 4

THE MYSTERY OF PRACTICING THE PRESENCE OF THE LORD

D O YOU KNOW what I want most as a believer? More and more of the presence of God.

I have discovered the essential keys that unlock the door to experiencing more of the presence of God. I am going to share these keys with you so that you can cross the threshold into a more dynamic life in God's presence.

Of course, the day I stand before the Lord Jesus, I want Him to look at me with a smile and say, "Well done." But while I'm still here on the earth, I want more and more of His presence. The Word of God clearly states that we are to seek the Lord with all our hearts—not half, not two-thirds, but with *all* our hearts.

> Blessed are they that keep his testimonies, and that seek him with the whole heart....With my whole heart have I sought thee: O let me not wander from thy commandments.
> —PSALM 119:2, 10

Seeking God with our whole hearts empowers us to keep His testimonies. The Hebrew word that is translated "testimonies" in Psalm 119:2 means God's *precepts*. A *precept* is a principle or rule that regulates behavior or thought. When we seek God with our whole hearts, it gives us the strength to not wander from His commandments. Seeking God with our whole hearts is a master key to practicing the presence of the Lord.

> And I will walk at liberty: for I seek thy precepts.
>
> —PSALM 119:45

Seeking God with our whole hearts requires time. The tangible presence of God is what we're after in our walk with Him because the presence of the Lord Jesus nourishes, protects, strengthens, and empowers our inner man. But it only becomes a reality when we spend time with Him. Time is the price we pay. God will not show up, His presence will not become tangible, if we do not set our hearts on giving Him our uninterrupted time.

Another key to unlocking the door to a life alive with God's presence is placing your focus upon the Lord. We cannot have divine communion and human communion at the same time—we absolutely cannot. I cannot stress this enough—you cannot pollute the waters of communication with the Lord and expect to get a pure drink of His presence. He will not allow it. He wants your full and undivided attention, your whole heart. If something sidetracks you, He will hold back or pull away altogether, and regaining His trust will be very difficult.

God will not share His time. For example, you're in the presence of God, and the phone rings, so you stop and answer it. The Lord will not manifest His presence if you answer that phone. The flow of communication will be disrupted by the interruption. He will hold back until you finish what you have to do or say, and you will have to make an effort to get back to the place where you were before you answered the phone. You will have wasted time by cutting the line of communication with God in favor of a line of communication with another human being.

Our God is a jealous God. He wants all the time that you put aside for Him. When you say to the Lord, "This is Your time," He wants all of it. He wants every minute of it. Every second of it belongs to Him. He will not manifest His presence if someone knocks on the door and you answer it. The God we serve is jealous. You must stop the distractions that will steal your focus from seeking the Lord with your whole heart.

> And ye shall seek me, and find me, when ye shall search for me with all your heart.
>
> —JEREMIAH 29:13

Another important key to practicing the presence of the Lord is spending time with God daily. It is absolutely vital that you set aside a period of uninterrupted time to commune daily with God. First Chronicles 16:10–11 says, "Glory ye in his holy name: let the heart of them rejoice that seek the LORD. Seek the LORD and his strength, seek his face continually." The Hebrew word translated here as "continually" could also be translated "daily."

I recommend spending at least an hour with the Lord every day. (If you are in full-time ministry, you need to spend more time than this, and I explain why in a later chapter.) Spending at least an hour a day with the Lord builds your relationship. It's like spending time with your spouse or a friend, whomever you build a relationship with. You get to know them more and more because you're spending time together. When you're trying to spend time with someone you love and that time gets interrupted by someone else, you get irritated because your alone time was cut short. You didn't get to connect as deeply as you wanted. The same is true when your time alone with the Lord is chopped in two.

I cannot overstate how important it is to build upon this daily. I find that if I miss a day, I go backward; I'm not at the same place I was before I missed my time with Him. The more I spend time with Him, the quicker I get into His presence; the less I spend time with Him, the slower I get in.

Sometimes you miss your time with God because something comes up and your schedule changes that day—you're traveling, or something distracts you. But you have to decide that nothing and no one will prevent you from having time with the Lord. I typically spend time with the Lord at 1:00 p.m., but if I miss that time, I'll do it at night. God is not concerned that you missed a specific time. He is concerned that you missed the day. Don't go to bed without giving the Lord the time that belongs to Him.

HOW TO SPEND YOUR TIME WITH GOD

Once you decide to spend time each day in the presence of the Lord, you may wonder what you're supposed to do during that time. Many people assume I spend the majority of that time praying. I spend much of my time waiting upon the Lord and worshipping. I wait upon the Lord to quicken me (Ps. 80:18). It might surprise you to read this, but I have come to believe that prayer in and of itself is not necessarily powerful. After all, religious people pray. Even well-meaning Christians try to put a spiritual label on things they are doing in the flesh, even spiritual practices such as prayer, fasting, and praise.

The problem is, there is no power in those things when they are done in the flesh. There is only power in the presence of Jesus. When we commune with the Lord, there is power. As we spend time with Jesus and He becomes real to us, there is real power.

There are two realms in which we operate: the realm of the flesh and the realm of the spirit. Only in the realm of the spirit will you see lasting results. There are no lasting results in the flesh; anything that seems like a result there is only temporary and will quickly disappear. What happens in the realm of the spirit is eternal. Second Corinthians 4:18 says, "...while we do not look at the things which are seen, but at the things which are not seen. For the things which are seen are temporary, but the things which are not seen are eternal" (NKJV).

We are to walk in the Spirit. Galatians 5:25 makes this very clear: "If we live in the Spirit, let us also walk in the Spirit." In other words, we need to get in the Spirit and live there.

People don't just naturally know how to live in the Spirit. They don't know how to find their way to that secret place. The secret place is the world God wants us to live in. Psalm 91:1 says, "He that *dwelleth* in the secret place of the most High shall abide under the shadow of the Almighty." It doesn't say, "He that visits the secret place." That's the problem. Too many people visit and then leave. Let's take another look at this scriptural promise: "He that dwelleth in the secret place...*shall abide*." That means it's your address, your place of residence. It's where you live.

How do you get there? Let me share what I've learned about it, and I sure have learned this the hard way. Now, you probably already know the key I'm about to give you, but you just don't practice it. Maybe you want to, but you just don't know how. The key is this: "They that wait upon the LORD shall renew their strength" (Isa. 40:31). Waiting upon the Lord is the secret. Waiting upon the Lord is the bridge between the flesh and the Spirit.

How do we wait? The Bible says very clearly that we are to be still. God never said, "Be quiet," because it's not enough to just be quiet. He said, "Be still." There's a big difference. Quietness is soulish. Stillness is spiritual. If you allow it, quietness will lead you to stillness. When you are quiet long enough, God will bring stillness to your spirit man. Let God quicken you to stillness. The Holy Spirit manifests Himself when we are still. Stillness activates His power. Stillness releases His power in us. Stillness manifests the presence of God in us. Stillness leads us to a deeper understanding of what it means to be in the presence of the living God.

In Psalm 46:10 God says, "Be still, and know that I am God." He is saying, "Be still, and then you will know who I am." He is saying, "Be still, and then you will know My presence." We don't know His presence because we do not want to be still. We think being still is hard because we have to sit there and do nothing. But we must change our thinking. We are not *doing nothing* because we are not *waiting on nothing*. We are waiting on the Lord. That's not *nothing*; it's a very important *something*. It's an action, or rather, an act of faith. Waiting on the Lord requires you to believe that while it seems as if you are idle, you are not wasting time. In reality you are actively communicating with the Lord.

Read this clearly: I am not saying you shouldn't pray. The Bible says we can make our requests known. But there comes a time when we finish our prayer lists. What do most people do when they're done asking God for things? They say amen and walk away. Imagine that—they are in active communication with the Creator of the universe, and they do all the talking and *none* of the listening! That is when they lose. That is the definition of *visiting* instead of *dwelling*. So when you finish your prayer list, be quiet long enough for God to quicken you, to ignite you.

> So will not we go back from thee: quicken us, and we will call upon thy name.
>
> —Psalm 80:18

> Draw me, we will run after thee: the king hath brought me into his chambers: we will be glad and rejoice in thee, we will remember thy love more than wine: the upright love thee.
>
> —Song of Solomon 1:4

When the Holy Spirit quickens you, He will bring you into the realm of the spirit. You cannot come in on your own just because you want to. You must be drawn in by the Holy Spirit. And how does it happen? ("They that wait upon the LORD shall renew their [spiritual] strength; they shall mount up with wings as eagles." The moment your spirit strengthens, the Holy Spirit quickens you, and when He quickens you, He brings you in "with wings as eagles.")

> But they that wait upon the LORD shall renew their strength; they shall mount up with wings as eagles; they shall run, and not be weary; and they shall walk, and not faint.
> —ISAIAH 40:31

I want to show you something very powerful about this truth. What does it mean to mount up with wings as eagles? It means knowing the currents of the winds of the Spirit. The eagle does not fly; the eagle *soars.* The eagle *surrenders* to the winds. It waits for the strongest winds and then surrenders. Waiting upon the Lord results in surrender to the Lord. And notice the following: "They shall run, and not be weary; and they shall walk, and not faint." In the Spirit we run before we walk. In other words, we run to catch up with God, and then we walk with Him.

Waiting upon the Lord disarms the flesh. It allows you time to forget about yourself and see Jesus. It dismantles the powers of sin. It gives you Holy Spirit strength in your inner man, and the flesh begins to lose its grip on your life. That is what Paul meant when he said, "I keep under my body, and bring it into subjection" (1 Cor. 9:27).

The minute you enter the realm of the spirit, something happens. Psalm 40:3 says, "He hath put a new song in my mouth, even praise unto our God." The realm of the spirit begins with a melody. You begin to sing songs in the Spirit. Now, you don't have to have music to get into the Spirit, but it may help. There's nothing wrong with playing worship music to change the atmosphere and keep you focused so you aren't distracted by other things.

I like to play worship music as I wait upon the Lord. I find that the more often you connect with God, the less you need the music. Sometimes it can be a blockage because once you are in the flow, you don't need anything from this earth. The only reason we need worship music is so we can calm our emotions, forget our troubles, and unite with the Lord Jesus without distractions. But the moment the Holy Spirit quickens you, that is all you need. That's when the Lord Jesus becomes real. The practice of the presence of the Lord begins when Jesus becomes more real to us than our problems, our families, our troubles, and even more real than life itself. At that moment, it is all about Jesus.

Chapter 5

THE MYSTERY OF IGNITING THE WORD AND WORSHIP

PRACTICING THE PRESENCE of the Lord deepens your intimacy with Him. Spending time with God is fuel for the engine of your soul that drives you to know Him (hunger), to walk with Him (faith), and to worship Him (love).

Remarkably, He gives you the hunger, faith, and love to walk with Him. The most valuable thing you and I have to give is our time. When you give God your time, something amazing happens: as the presence of the Lord manifests because of time spent with Him, the Word of God suddenly takes hold of your soul.

As you give the Lord your time, the Holy Spirit captures you with His Word. You find that when you read the Word, it comes right off the pages and takes hold of your heart. You are drawn into it like never before. Your hunger and faith explode to new levels, and this explosion creates new levels of spiritual growth. Because you give your time, the Holy Spirit uses His Word to draw you in. When that happens, it's like an ignition that revs up your soul with combustible power. You are taken into a world you didn't know existed. When you open your heart and open your Bible, you unlock the exciting new universe of God's Word.

You can now go into deeper levels of the Word of God, as the

Word of God begins to saturate you. His Word begins to cleanse your mind and purify your heart.

> ...as Christ also loved the church, and gave himself for it; that he might sanctify and cleanse it with the washing of water by the word...
>
> —Ephesians 5:25–26

His Word begins to govern your thought life as everything in you begins to come into alignment with God's purpose and plan for your life, found on the precious pages of God's written Word. Something begins to happen to you spiritually as you are pulled into the depths of God and His Word.

When hunger, faith, and love begin to manifest in your life, they trigger the Word in you at a deeper level than before. That's what Paul meant by "the power that worketh in us" (Eph. 3:20). It triggers the Word. The Word ignites communion and fellowship. In turn, communion ignites worship. The three ignitions of the Christian life are the Word, communion, and worship. Once they are activated, they intensify, being ignited by each other. This combustion begins a kind of chain reaction in your spirit, reigniting again and again as you remain in the presence of the Lord.

Once that anointing begins to ignite, the spirit man starts to experience the abundant tangibility of it. You have probably experienced the first stages of this without realizing it. If you go a little deeper, here's what could happen: when you go into the depths, the ignitions become very powerful. Suddenly you find yourself going into deeper layers of the Scriptures.

I didn't discover that the Bible has layers until I had been in the ministry for five years. The first layer is historical. The second layer is God's plan for Israel and the church. The third layer is where you discover Jesus in the pages of the Old Testament. That's when the ignition hits on all cylinders!

How many times can you read about Adam and Eve, Abraham, Isaac, Jacob, Noah and the ark, Joseph and his brothers, and Moses? These individuals and events can sometimes be stored in our minds as mere information. But something significant happens the second we discover Jesus in the pages of our Bibles. This ignites power! The ignition doesn't begin when you're in the historical layer. The ignition doesn't take place when you're discovering God's plan for the nation of Israel and the church. But the second you go deep—and you cannot go deep without the Holy Spirit showing it to you—that is when you discover Jesus in the revelation of Scripture.

The Bible is not just about history or poetry or prophecy. The Bible is a revelation of one person: Jesus, the Son of God. Seeing Jesus on every page of the Bible is what transforms us into His image.

It took me five years to even discover that this existed. Suddenly I realized Adam's being put to sleep has nothing to do with Adam. It is the revelation of Jesus dying on the cross. Why did God put Adam to sleep? To bring forth his wife. Why did Jesus die on the cross? To bring forth His bride, the church. God opened Adam's side for his bride, Eve, to come forth, which reveals that the side of Jesus had to open for His bride, the church, to come forth.

Then I began to see that Joseph is not about Joseph. He was loved by his father. That's Jesus. He was hated by his brothers. That's Jesus. He was placed in a pit, which is the death of Jesus. He was placed in a prison, which is Jesus in the underworld. He came out of prison, and that's the resurrection. He was seated at Pharaoh's right hand, and that's the ascension. He was given a Gentile wife, and that's the church. Suddenly, Joseph is no longer Joseph. It's all about Jesus.

Even the feasts of Israel are revelations of the Lord Jesus, His life and ministry.

1. The Feast of the Passover—His death on the cross

2. The Feast of Unleavened Bread—when Jesus took our sins upon Himself

3. The Feast of Firstfruits—the Lord's resurrection from the dead

4. The Feast of Weeks (Pentecost)—the coming of the Holy Spirit on the day of Pentecost

5. The Feast of Trumpets—the rapture of the church

6. The Day of Atonement—the salvation of Israel

7. The Feast of Tabernacles—the millennium reign of Christ Jesus

It's all about Jesus!

I encourage you to go deep in the Bible like this because it ignites great power and you begin to live in God's blessings and favor; you begin to experience your destiny. The Lord begins to manifest Himself. There is growth and a renewal of the mind.

> And be not conformed to this world; but be ye transformed
> by the renewing of your mind, that ye may prove what is
> that good, and acceptable, and perfect, will of God.
> —ROMANS 12:2

Amazing things happen when you move deeper in the Word. First, there is a quietness that invades and permeates you. It is a solemn, sacred experience. The abiding anointing *stills* the soul, while the empowering anointing *stirs* the soul. Second, moving deeper in the Word creates depth in your communion with the Lord. Third, worship erupts on a level you've never known before. Deep communion ignites dynamic, explosive worship!

When worship erupts, God's presence manifests and becomes

tangible to us. His *dunamis* power begins to work in us, bringing us to that place Paul talked about in Ephesians 3:20 when he said, "exceeding abundantly above all that we ask or think." That tangible presence of the Lord begins to transform you into His image.

As you practice the presence, three things happen:

1. God increases your hunger, faith, and love for Him.

2. Power explodes in you, bringing you into the depths of the Word where the Lord reveals Himself to you.

3. Dynamic worship in the Spirit ignites and brings the transformation of the Lord into your life. Now you are transformed from glory to glory. The transformation from your image into the Lord's image begins at this point and will be complete when we see His precious face on that glorious day!

Developing deep fellowship with God is imperative, yet it seems so basic that many Christians overlook it. If you take nothing else from this book, please learn this: you cannot afford to neglect spending time with God. This is where you develop a deep fellowship with Him. It is essential because it builds a mighty foundation under you. When God begins to use you in your call to Christian ministry, that foundation of fellowship is your anchor. You are built upon the rock, Christ Jesus. You're not built upon sinking sand. That daily time of deep fellowship is building your life on the Lord and His Word.

Eventually the Lord will begin to trust you with the empowering anointing for ministry. Your ministry is the result of the walk I've been writing about. Because you've given Him your time and grown through divine Word revelations and intense worship, God's presence is tangible in your life. That's when God says, "I can trust you," and He anoints you with the empowering anointing of Acts 1:8. Then the gifts of the Spirit come alive because of the empowering anointing upon your life.

That's what the Bible means by *dunamis* power; it's a power that ignites itself. The English words *dynamo* and *dynamite* come from the Greek word *dunamis*. The purpose of this Holy Ghost *dunamis* within you is to touch others with God's power. When the woman with the issue of blood recorded in the eighth chapter of Luke touched the hem of Jesus' garment, He said, "Who touched Me?" Virtue, strength, and power flowed out of Him. The word used there is from that same Greek word, *dunamis*. The release of that power made this woman whole.

Worship is so intense it ignites the Word; then the Word ignites revelation and worship, and it just keeps going back and forth in a spiritual chain reaction. This chain reaction is what brings you into a place of total transformation where God begins to re-create your image into His.

Chapter 6

THE MYSTERY OF TOTAL TRANSFORMATION

VERY FEW PEOPLE have gotten to the place of total transformation, perhaps because there aren't many willing to pay the price. But before the Lord takes me home, I want to get there.

A young pastor from Nigeria once asked me a powerful question. He said, "Is it possible to become one with God, and have you known people who were one with God?" I told him that of course it's possible because that was the prayer of the Lord in John chapter 17.

> Neither pray I for these alone, but for them also which shall believe on me through their word; that they all may be one; as thou, Father, art in me, and I in thee, that they also may be one in us: that the world may believe that thou hast sent me.
>
> —JOHN 17:20–21

I have known of three people who were one with God. All of them were women: Basilea Schlink, Corrie ten Boom, and Kathryn Kuhlman. Let me tell you a little about each of them.

Basilea Schlink

Basilea Schlink was born in Germany in 1904. Her university studies included a thesis on sin consciousness and its effect on faith. A leader in the Student Christian Movement, she came under investigation by the Nazis during World War II for her stand in defense of the Jews. After the war ended, Schlink understood the importance of repentance for the atrocities committed by her homeland. She decided instead of marrying, she would remain single and devote her life to Christ. In 1947 she cofounded The Evangelical Sisterhood of Mary and served there until her death in 2001, sharing her faith with others and authoring ten books.

When David Wilkerson went to see Basilea Schlink, he said he could not even get in the room. He began to weep when he came near her. I've heard her teachings, but I never met her. But while she was alive, I went to the place she founded, called Canaan, in Darmstadt, Germany. The presence of the Lord in that place was so powerful that I began to weep. I went to the chapel, and I did not want to walk out. It was like being in heaven inside that chapel. It was empty, but the presence of God in that place was so glorious, so real, that it felt as if I had gone to heaven and was walking with the Lord in glory. I felt that presence because Basilea Schlink walked in total transformation. She knew the Lord and was one with the Lord.

Corrie ten Boom

Corrie ten Boom was born in the Netherlands in 1892. A watchmaker by trade, following in her father's profession, she was part of the Dutch Reformed Church and served the people of her neighborhood and established a youth club. After Germany invaded the Netherlands in World War II, youth clubs were banned and Jews were persecuted. The ten Boom family took in Jewish refugees, hiding them from the Nazis. For this, she and other members of her family were arrested; she and her family were confined in German concentration camps. Some did not survive the war, but she did. She shared the story of her family in *The Hiding Place* and wrote a number of other books as she traveled the world, sharing her message of hope, love, and forgiveness through Christ Jesus until her death in 1983.

I met Corrie ten Boom and danced with her. I was with her in her home, and we were in the garden dancing. I was nineteen years old at the time, and I was friends with her nephew. We were roommates. God has graced my life to know all those people in a way. When ten Boom preached, her face glowed, and I was mesmerized that Jesus walked into the room when that lady walked on the platform. Like Basilea Schlink, ten Boom had become one with the Lord.

Kathryn Kuhlman

Kathryn Kuhlman was born in Missouri in 1907. She began preaching at the age of fourteen, traveling with her older sister and brother-in-law. In the 1940s she began holding healing crusades and continued her crusades into the 1970s. Her weekly television program, *I Believe in Miracles*, extended her ministry's outreach, and she authored several books over these years. An estimated two million people reported healings through her ministry. She was diagnosed with a heart problem in her late forties but refused to allow this to impact her ministry. In spite of sometimes debilitating pain in her chest, she continued her ministry, both in person and on television. She died during open-heart surgery in 1976. It was documented that at the moment of her death the doctors and nurses in attendance saw a bright light hover over her lifeless body for a moment before it vanished.

Kathryn Kuhlman embodied total transformation and oneness with the Lord. I can't tell you how often I sat in her meetings at First Presbyterian Church of Pittsburgh and saw her face glowing. The presence of the Lord was manifested within her in such a glorious way that it is difficult to describe in words. This total transformation made Jesus a reality in her daily life. When Kuhlman walked on the platform, the reality of Christ in her life was now in the whole building. The presence of Christ Jesus saturated the entire place, and it immersed everyone in it.

The same thing happened in her large meetings. When the Lord became real to her, everything in the audience changed. When Jesus became real, the whole place came alive. He was already real in her life. Now He suddenly became real to the whole crowd, many of whom didn't even know Him. In her meetings people were caught up in the reality that she lived in. Her reality made Him real to the crowd and created a hunger where people would say, "I want to know Him like this." That's what happened to me.

Now think about what would have happened if there were no such reality of Jesus in her life when she walked onto the platform. The crowd would have gotten entertainment, signs, wonders, and good preaching, but those things can't change us. The reality of the Lord Jesus is what changes us. The reality *in* Ms. Kuhlman's life combined with the power *on* her, and when she walked on the platform, the power *on* her transmitted the reality *in* her.

My ongoing prayer is that the same experience happens when I minister. If the Lord Jesus isn't there, it doesn't matter if people think, "Oh, that Pastor Benny, we all love him. He's a good man. He's a good Bible teacher." If all they can say later is, "Well, I learned something, but I wasn't changed," what was the point? But when the Lord Jesus is in that audience, that's what makes all the difference. Who cares if I ever preach? I just want to bring Jesus with me because that's when lives are changed.

In this book I am giving you the foundation of life and ministry. It culminates with total transformation where the power *on* you is the transmitter of the presence *in* you. And when the power of God comes on you, it transmits what's inside you to everyone around you. They sense it; they feel it; they become part of it.

Chapter 7

GOD'S ROAD MAP INTO HIS PRESENCE

G OD GAVE MOSES the road map into His presence. This road map is more than a historical account of a Jewish religious custom. This is a relevant road map of the biblical protocol and pattern we follow to access the presence of Jehovah God. The Old Testament tabernacle shows us the seven practices of the presence of God. When God gave Moses the plans for the tabernacle in Exodus 25–31, He told him where to place the gate, the altar of sacrifice, the laver, the lampstand, the table of shewbread, the altar of incense, and the ark of the covenant. These represent the seven manifestations of the practices of God's presence. I'll show you.

When you begin to commune and fellowship with Jesus by practicing His presence, you have entered through the gate. You have entered the realm of the spirit, because it's impossible to experience His presence from outside. Suddenly, Jesus is real. And when Jesus is real, faith is born. You don't need to seek faith; you only need to seek Jesus, and He'll give you the faith.

Let me share special insight and clarity on something very important. People have gotten off track by seeking faith instead of seeking *Jesus*. Sometimes people confess scriptures and claim healings, but nothing happens. This is because they have not waited upon the Lord first. They have not waited for His Holy Spirit to move. Genesis 1 says first the Spirit moved, and _then_ God spoke. God always speaks into the wind of the Spirit. He always speaks _after_ the Spirit moves. When you don't enter the spirit realm first and wait for God to speak, even things you do that seem spiritual are being done in the flesh, and they produce no lasting results.

You and I can only enter the spirit realm by waiting upon the Lord. It may take a half hour, an hour, or even longer, but this time will not be wasted. As we wait, we are quickened, and when we are quickened, Jesus becomes real. When Jesus becomes real, a song is born. And when a song is born, something happens. We come to the altar of sacrifice, where the blood of Jesus becomes more real than our bondage. At that moment, as we are practicing the presence of the Lord, our hearts break open. His Word says, "The sacrifices of God are a broken spirit: a broken and a contrite heart, O God, thou wilt not despise" (Ps. 51:17). There is brokenness, repentance, cleansing, and forgiveness. "Old things are passed away" (2 Cor. 5:17), and the very memory of sin is gone from our souls.

Let me share something many people miss: A lot of people confess their sins in the flesh. That's why they go back and sin again. But when you repent in the Spirit, it is impossible to repeat the same sinful behavior because the Holy Spirit erases it.

The third place you come to in the practice of the presence of the Lord is the Word. That's the laver in the tabernacle, the place where those who served the Lord washed, and it is here that we wash ourselves with the Word. This is the place where the promises of God suddenly become powerful. Now you can look up and say, "Father, Your Word says...," and you take hold of that promise. Because you're in the Spirit, there's a confidence, just as

John talked about when he said, "This is the confidence that we have in him, that, if we ask any thing according to his will, he heareth us" (1 John 5:14). How do you know He's heard you? You know because you are in the Spirit. If you are in the flesh, you will question whether God hears you. But when you are in the Spirit, you know He has heard you. And then you know you have what you have requested of the Lord.

Then you move into the holy place, another level of the practice of God's presence, and you come to the lampstand, which is the renewal of the mind that has been enlightened by God. It is where you know His will; the Light allows us to see what we could not discern before. You see, at the gate Jesus becomes real. At the altar of sacrifice the cross becomes real. At the laver the Word becomes real. At the lampstand His will becomes real. He reveals His will. You know His plans for your life, and you join in. *His will becomes your will.*

Across the way is the table of shewbread, and that's where you present your body as a living sacrifice. The bread is the body. Jesus said, "This is my body," when He gave them the bread at the last supper. The bread speaks of the body being surrendered to Him. That's where we yield our members as instruments of righteousness. That is where we offer Him that living sacrifice. The greatest experience in the baptism of the Spirit is when we give Him our bodies as living sacrifices, and our bodies become His body.

> I beseech you therefore, brethren, by the mercies of God,
> that ye present your bodies a living sacrifice, holy, accept-
> able unto God, which is your reasonable service.
>
> —ROMANS 12:1

Then you come to the blessed altar of incense, which is worship. What is worship? Worship is intimacy and union with the Lord. You are in communion with the Master. It's where you enter in and He takes hold of you. Every cell in your body adores Him. Every part of your being magnifies His name. It's not mental; this is totally spiritual. It's where "deep calleth unto deep at the noise of thy waterspouts" (Ps. 42:7). The verse continues, "Thy waves and thy billows are gone over me." This verse describes great depth in the Spirit. Those waterspouts are tornadoes in the ocean. Think about the Holy Spirit lifting you in the water and bringing a wave of such power and glory on your life that you will be completely immersed in the presence of the Lord.

When this happens, worship will explode inside your being. In that worship, you will hear God's voice, and that is the ark of the covenant in the holy of holies. You enter into the most sacred of all places in the practice of God's presence. "He that dwelleth in the secret place of the most High shall abide under the shadow of the Almighty" (Ps. 91:1). This is our hiding place. Verse 2 says, "I will say of the LORD, He is my refuge and my fortress: my God; in him will I trust." Next we look at verses 7–8: "A thousand shall fall at thy side, and ten thousand at thy right hand; but it shall not come nigh thee. Only with thine eyes shalt thou behold and see the reward of the wicked." And verse 10 says, "There shall no evil befall thee, neither shall any plague come nigh thy dwelling." Why? Because you dwell in the shelter of the most High! You are in there! Now that you have spent time in that blessed place, the glory of God has wrapped itself around you.

Can I tell you something? When I used to go to Kathryn Kuhlman's meetings, I always wondered how she could walk out on the platform without saying a word, and people would be healed. I was amazed by it. I couldn't understand how she just stood there without saying a word or preaching a message and people were healed. I now know why.

When you experience the depth of communion that she

experienced, Jesus walks into the room with you.) Your presence becomes His presence. Your vessel becomes His vessel. You carry that glory in you wherever you are. When you arrive, the presence of God arrives with you because you have become one with Him.

I remember a time when Kathryn Kuhlman came to London, Ontario, for a miracle service. Many of us from our church in Toronto traveled to her meeting together. We had a bus full of excited people as we pulled up in front of the Holiday Inn to check in before the miracle service that night. As we entered the lobby, we sensed the presence of the Lord Jesus in a very strong way. I was amazed and wondered why we sensed the Lord's presence, because the miracle service was to be at the stadium, not at the Holiday Inn. As we were checking in, the elevator door opened, and we were stunned to see Ms. Kuhlman exit the elevator with her assistant, Maggie Hartner. They walked through the lobby and went outside to wait for a cab while all of us looked on in amazement, still sensing the presence of Jesus. When the cab drove off with Ms. Kuhlman, the glory lifted from the hotel lobby. Imagine living so close to the Master that you carry Him with you everywhere you go. This is my greatest longing.

The practice of the presence of God is the realm of the spirit, and in the realm of the spirit the promises of God are activated. In the realm of the spirit, victory comes to you. You can't win over your sin outside of that realm. It is impossible. Because the Bible says, "For the law of the Spirit of life in Christ Jesus [which means in the Spirit] hath made me free from the law of sin and death" (Rom. 8:2). You cannot truly know the love of God without that realm.

> For I am persuaded, that neither death, nor life, nor angels,
> nor principalities, nor powers, nor things present, nor things
> to come, nor height, nor depth, nor any other creature, shall

be able to separate us from the love of God, *which is in Christ Jesus our Lord.*

—Romans 8:38–39

The minute you are in Christ in the spirit, His love is real. "[Pray] always with all prayer and supplication *in the Spirit*" (Eph. 6:18). You enter in as He quickens you, and at the gate you experience Jesus. At the altar you experience His blood, and at the laver His Word. You learn His will at the lampstand. Then you surrender at the table of shewbread, and He takes over your vessel. Lastly, you worship at the altar of incense, and His glory wraps around you as you experience the ark of the covenant where He speaks to you. And now you walk out, and He will come with you.

In that secret place is your safety. Outside of that secret place is danger. Let's look at what David said about it under the anointing of the Spirit in Psalm 32:7.

Thou art my hiding place; thou shalt preserve me from trouble; thou shalt compass me about with songs of deliverance.

This is what happens in the secret place. There is safety. Today, with all the fear out in the world, new pestilences and new threats, you might be tempted to wonder what kind of world your children and grandchildren will live in. I have these thoughts too. But the Lord assures me that they will be just fine if they remain in the secret place. They will be protected. We will also be protected as we remain in the secret place.

Be merciful unto me, O God, be merciful unto me: for my soul trusteth in thee: yea, in the shadow of thy wings will I make my refuge, until these calamities be overpast.

—Psalm 57:1

What I've written so far is the foundation that will keep you safe in His arms. In the coming pages I want to deal with the anointing that comes on you for ministry, how different it is from the one in you, and how both can work together to bring about the most amazing revelation of the Lord to a world that desperately needs Him.

PART II

ANOINTED FOR MINISTRY

Chapter 8

THE MYSTERY OF THE EMPOWERING ANOINTING

THE EMPOWERING ANOINTING is a topic many believers are completely unaware of. Yet if you are a child of God, cleansed by the blood of Jesus and sealed by His Spirit, you can and should operate with the empowering anointing. Remember, the abiding anointing of 1 John 2:27 is *in* you, and the empowering anointing of Acts 1:8 is *on* you. They are separate. Many believers are not even aware of the Holy Spirit's activity in their lives, let alone the different types of anointing. But if you desire to be used by God, it is essential to understand how to operate in the empowering anointing.

Not everyone is called to stand behind a pulpit or hold an office of apostle, prophet, evangelist, pastor, or teacher. But every Christian can and should have a ministry—whether it is interceding in prayer to fight spiritual battles, witnessing to others and leading them to Christ, laying hands on people to pray for healing, the working of miracles, ministering to others through words of knowledge or other spiritual gifts, or the ministry of helps. And if you are going to be used by God to minister to others, you must have the empowering anointing.

I have found David my servant; with my holy oil have I anointed him.

—PSALM 89:20

BUILDING UPON THE ABIDING ANOINTING

The empowering anointing should be built upon the sure foundation of the abiding anointing. Let's start by taking another look at Acts 1:8.

But ye shall receive power, after that the Holy Ghost is come *upon* you: and ye shall be witnesses unto me.

It may surprise you to learn that the empowering anointing *upon* you is not *about* you. It's not about you because you cannot earn it or achieve it on your own. It's not about you because it is not for your personal benefit. It is for the benefit of others. It's not about you because it's about Him. It is about the Lord Jesus. The empowering anointing is for God's glory. *It's not about you.*

The abiding anointing that He has placed in you is completely under God's control. He is totally in charge of it. As long as you are walking with the Lord and abiding in His presence, you are living in the fullness of this anointing within you. It has one main purpose: to transform you into the image of the Lord. That's it.

That's the excitement of the Christian life. It is about so much more than just your being on your way to heaven. What makes the Christian life so exciting is that you are continually becoming more like Jesus. The change began on the day you were saved, and since then you have been becoming more and more like Jesus every day. As long as you remain here on this earth, you will continue to be transformed into the image of Christ Jesus. That's what the abiding anointing does.

CONTRASTING THE ABIDING AND EMPOWERING ANOINTINGS

Every Christian receives the abiding anointing at the moment of salvation, but not every Christian receives the empowering anointing. God reserves the empowering anointing for those He uses in ministry. It is received only after we have grown in intimacy with the Lord and He trusts us.

The abiding anointing, within you, builds you spiritually; how strongly it operates depends on your own hunger. But the empowering anointing, which is *upon* you, relies mainly on the hunger of the people to whom you minister. As a result of *their* hunger for the power of God, He begins to fill you with everything that they need. They may need miracles. Some may need deliverance. Many will need healing. Now the burden of ministry becomes very heavy because of the needs of the people, and if you tried to carry it under your own power, you would fall and it would crush you.

> Not by might, nor by power, but by my spirit, saith the LORD of hosts.
>
> —ZECHARIAH 4:6

If you are spending time daily in deep communion with the Lord, you will be strong enough to bear this burden. If you fail to spend time in His presence, this burden will be too great for you to bear and you will not want to even make an attempt to carry it anymore.

If you are to be used by God in any ministry capacity, the empowering anointing is essential. This vital equipping enables you to work for the Lord and fulfill your purpose in the ministry to which God has called you. Believe me when I say, you do not want to be in ministry without the empowerment of the

Holy Spirit. Perfect sermons without the anointing fall power-less to the floor. The world's most talented singers without the anointing have never changed one life. It's the anointing that makes the difference.

THE DANGERS OF THE EMPOWERING ANOINTING

Now I will write about something you will never learn in Bible school: the dangers of the empowering anointing. This is not a subject that is taught in classrooms or preached from pulpits. But there are genuine dangers, and you can do a lot of damage to yourself, your family, and the people you minister to if you do not properly handle the empowering anointing.

Let's look at what the prophet Samuel said to Saul.

> And the Spirit of the LORD will come upon thee, and thou shalt prophesy with them, and shalt be turned into another man. And let it be, when these signs are come unto thee, *that thou do as occasion serve thee*; for God is with thee.
>
> —1 SAMUEL 10:6–7

First, note that it says, "the Spirit of the LORD will come upon thee"—*upon* thee, not *in* thee. So we know this is the outer anointing, the empowering anointing. Next, notice verse 7 says, "...that thou do as occasion serve thee." This is why there are dangers: you are now in charge. God is in charge of the abiding anointing, the one that grows and deepens as you fellowship with Him. But you are in charge of the empowering anointing, which comes upon you for ministry to others. God controls the anointing *in* you; you control the anointing *on* you. You can use it or abuse it. You can use it to bless people or misuse it and harm people.

You must get this. It is vital that you understand this. Most people miss it. Verse 7 says, "Do as occasion serves you." This means do whatever comes to your spirit as you serve in ministry. Now that the empowering anointing is yours, do as you feel led to do.

When God places the empowering anointing upon you, He is trusting you with this divine equipping. He trusts you with it so much that He puts *you* in charge of it. Think about how amazing that is! He is in charge of the abiding anointing, which transforms you, yet He puts *you* in charge of the empowering anointing, which demonstrates His power to the world!

What makes the empowering anointing so amazing is the same thing that makes it so dangerous: God puts us in charge of it. If you are not careful, that level of power can quickly and easily go right to your head. You can do great damage with it. And sadly, many have.

What will you do with the empowering anointing? Many will be rejected because they didn't use it properly. The Lord calls them workers of iniquity and says, "I never knew you" (Matt. 7:23). We know this is true because we've seen people who have casually played with the empowering anointing. They've muddled this holy endowment with fleshly ambition, creating careers instead of callings. They've used it to manipulate others, to make money. They've turned it into cheap merchandise and put it up for sale.

The empowering anointing is a precious gift. We should respect it and hold it in awe, handling it with reverence. Many have lost a holy fear of handling the empowering anointing. This is a dangerous mistake; it is not to be taken lightly. God has trusted you with His tremendous power. You had better know what you're doing with it and treat it properly. I write this because I do not want you to hurt others or yourself with the gift that God has given you. Mishandling the anointing of God has brought great harm to so many; some have died. Just ask Uzzah. Uzzah was the son of Abinadab, in whose house the ark of the covenant had been placed when it was brought back from the land of the Philistines. I believe Uzzah became too comfortable with the ark of the covenant in his home and began to treat it casually. We must always revere God's holy presence and respect the empowering anointing that rests upon us.

> And when they came to Nachon's threshingfloor, Uzzah put forth his hand to the ark of God, and took hold of it; for the oxen shook it. And the anger of the LORD was kindled against Uzzah; and God smote him there for his error; and there he died by the ark of God.
>
> —2 SAMUEL 6:6–7

If someone improperly uses the empowering anointing, one can damage his own life. He can bring destruction to his soul. Remember what I said in chapter 3? This empowering anointing that comes upon you does not protect you from deception. Your inner anointing, the abiding anointing, is the one that protects you from deception, but if you neglect nourishing the abiding anointing, you can be deceived and mishandle the empowering anointing that comes upon you. You can misuse the Lord's name and His anointing. That is why Matthew 7:22–24 says in that day, many will say, "Lord, Lord, have we not prophesied in thy name? And in thy name have cast out devils? And in thy name done many wonderful works?" But He will say, "I never knew you."

Chapter 9

THE EMPOWERING ANOINTING GROWS AND MULTIPLIES

A S THE EMPOWERING anointing grows and multiplies, the gift of faith begins to operate. Remember what I wrote earlier about the different kinds of faith: the measure of faith is given with salvation, the fruit of faith is the result of salvation, and the gift of faith is the gift of ministry. That's when God is using you in ministry.

We see this progression in the Book of Acts. In Acts 2:47 Scripture shows us that the Lord added, in Acts 6:1 He multiplied, and in Acts 6:7 He multiplied greatly. So there is growth in the empowering anointing. We go from addition to multiplication to great multiplication. After that we don't even read about head counts or numbers. The Scripture just says multitudes, multitudes, multitudes. Why? Because now it was a massive ocean of believers. That's how the empowering anointing grows—it goes from addition to multiplication to great multiplication.

Now let me show you some things that can cause the empowering anointing to increase and intensify.

1.

THE WORD OF GOD

The Word of God is the first thing that will increase the anointing. Job 29:6 says, "...when I washed my steps with butter, and the rock poured me out rivers of oil." I've taught on this, but it can be hard for people to grasp. Washing your steps with butter refers to the depth of the Word of God. The depth of God's Word is not known by surface-reading three chapters a day. You do not find the depth of God's Word by speed-reading through the entire Bible. You do not grasp it simply by completing a "Read the Bible in a Year" plan.

Please understand, it is good to read through the entire Bible, and I highly recommend it, but that isn't the point here. Sailboats skim the surface of the water quickly, but the surface is the only place for them. Submarines get beneath the surface, even as far as the bottom in some instances. But depending on the materials and construction, there are limits to how deep a submarine may go. Only a deep-submergence vehicle, or DSV, can reach into the true depths of the ocean, plunging into the trenches and exploring places that were previously unable to be examined by man.

So it is with the Word of God. What I want to impress upon you is that just casually reading the Scripture is insufficient if you are seeking to attain the deep places of God's Word. Mere reading can be shallow and is only able to produce a weak, ankle-deep understanding of God's Word. To experience its depth, you have to study it, search it, go deep, deep, deep in the Scripture, examine its trenches.

If you want to discover the buried treasure hidden in God's Word, you will need precision tools to excavate the riches of the Holy Scriptures. Dig into the meaning of the Hebrew and Greek words and get to know what the Bible really says. You can do this by using some study tools; *Strong's Concordance* and an Amplified

Bible or other translation may be helpful. A Bible app or online study guide may provide multiple translations and study tools for easy access. These tools will help you view Scripture through a wider lens and see the details and take in a larger scope of God's precious Word.

Let me share a time when this happened to me. Years ago in Orlando, Florida, the anointing came upon my life in a massive way when I looked up from where I was sitting and I said, "Dear Jesus, give me a revelation of the blood." I felt such power when I said that. So I began studying the blood throughout the Word of God. I'd been reading the Bible, but our whole ministry took off when I began to *study* the Bible. The church began to grow like wildfire.

The Bible says, "Study to shew thyself approved unto God" (2 Tim. 2:15). Today, it's so much easier with the internet than what I did back in the seventies and eighties. Back then I had books on the floor, and my eyes were hurting; I was in pain physically. I would have to go and stretch and get back on the floor because there was no space on any table for all the books I had. They were spread all over the floor. I would lock myself in for hours and days. This is no exaggeration. But the anointing came. The empowering anointing comes when you pay the price. When you are willing to pay the price by studying God's eternal Word, the empowering anointing will come.

> Study to shew thyself approved unto God, a workman that needeth not to be ashamed, rightly dividing the word of truth.
>
> —2 Timothy 2:15

The Blood of Jesus

The blood of Jesus is the second truth the Bible says will keep the anointing growing in intensity. If one does not remain under the cleansing flow of the blood of Jesus, one day the empowering anointing can destroy that individual because he or she is not clean. Those who operate in ministry must maintain an upright life. Ruth 3:3 says, "Wash thyself therefore, and anoint thee." These are the words of Naomi, who was telling Ruth to first wash and then anoint herself. This means that first, the blood washes you, and then you can be anointed for God's service. The blood of Jesus keeps you intense in the empowering anointing of God. It keeps the intensity upon your ministry.

3 Fellowship With God

The third thing that will cause an increase, or expansion, of the empowering anointing in your life is fellowship with God, which is continual prayer. Smith Wigglesworth said, "I don't often spend more than half an hour in prayer, but I never go more than half an hour without praying."[1]

You will not receive the empowering anointing just by praying a few minutes a day. It takes more effort, more determination, more staying power. In Acts 1:4 the Lord Jesus told His followers to wait in Jerusalem, and the Word says in verse 14, "These all continued...in prayer." They continued, and then, in Acts 2, the power fell. It takes an ongoing, concerted prayer to reach this level. You cannot receive the power promised in Acts 2:4 without first practicing the continuing prayer of Acts 1:14.

4 Association With Other Anointed Men and Women

The Word of God, the blood of Jesus, and continued prayer intensify the empowering anointing. (But don't forget the life-changing, ministry-launching power of the right associations.) Right associations with other anointed men and women of God absolutely intensify the empowering anointing. Just ask Joshua.

Joshua was a man who loved the Word. He never left the tabernacle. He embraced God's Law and loved to fellowship with God. But Joshua also understood not to leave Moses. He knew if he left Moses, he would lose this God-ordained association.

In my case I don't know how I knew this, but I knew it, and I saw the results in my life even after I became an evangelist and pastor. I began preaching as an evangelist in 1974, I became a pastor in 1983, but long before that, something in me told me not to disconnect from Kathryn Kuhlman's ministry.

I would listen to her daily on the radio at precisely 8:00 p.m. Her broadcast came from Wheeling, West Virginia. I was taking notes in Toronto. I could hardly even hear the station because it was so far away. But it didn't matter. I was compelled to listen to Ms. Kuhlman. I still listen to recordings of her now. You might ask, "Why?" *Connection.*

Maybe for you it is reading books by Andrew Murray or other great Christian leaders. Maybe it is recording your favorite Christian program while you are at work so you can watch it and savor it when you are free to concentrate. When you read or watch or listen to the men and women of God you feel led to connect with, you will feel their anointing no matter where you are. Even if they are already in heaven, you will still feel the anointing while you are on the earth. Not only does the Lord anoint the individuals; He anoints their ministries. When a minister goes to heaven, the empowering anointing upon his or her ministry continues touching lives on earth through the minister's recordings, videos, and books. The anointing adheres to the printed page; it rides on the airwaves of a broadcast. If the anointing was flowing when the pages were penned or when the sermon or song was written, you will still feel it. The anointing is not limited by time or space. It does its work whenever and wherever God needs it to.

I have learned from personal experience the importance of

remaining associated with anointed men and women of God. My fellowship with God grows when I walk with Him. His presence deepens as I remain in communion with Him. But the empowering anointing develops and expands when I remain walking closely with God and connected to men and women whom God is using. Fellowship with those God uses is essential. Fellowship with God *and with His saints* is the key. (Hebrews 10:25 says, "...not forsaking the assembling of ourselves together." Don't neglect the powerful principle of staying connected to those who minister in the empowering anointing. Ecclesiastes 4 underlines this powerful principle.

> Two are better than one; because they have a good reward for their labour. For if they fall, the one will lift up his fellow....And if one prevail against him, two shall withstand him; and a threefold cord is not quickly broken.
>
> —ECCLESIASTES 4:9–10, 12

You by yourself are mighty through God. *You* can do all things through Christ who strengthens you. No weapon formed against *you* shall prosper. Greater is He that is in *you* than he that is in the world.

One can put one thousand to flight—one thousand. One thousand is a lot. But two can put ten thousand to flight. In the world one plus one equals two. In the kingdom one plus one equals ten thousand. With that kind of math, one can put one thousand to flight, two can put ten thousand to flight, three can put one hundred thousand to flight, and four can put a million to flight. We are stronger together.

> Again I say unto you, that if two of you shall agree on earth as touching any thing that they shall ask, it shall be done for them of my Father which is in heaven. For where two or

three are gathered together in my name, there am I in the midst of them.

—MATTHEW 18:19–20

Association with men and women of God is essential for the ministry. It intensifies the empowering anointing.

THE EMPOWERING ANOINTING IS FELT

You can *feel* the empowering anointing. The empowering anointing affects your emotions, your physical body. It doesn't affect your spirit or your spirit man. The abiding anointing *within* affects your spirit. The empowering anointing *on* you affects your physical body and your feelings. That's why when you are under it, you become emotional. You become stronger physically. First Samuel 10:6 says, "Thou...shalt be turned into another man." When the Spirit comes upon you, you will become a different person. You will talk differently, act differently, think differently, and feel different. Everything about you is different.

When the empowering anointing rests upon you, you may become uncharacteristically loud, demonstrative, emotional, or sensitive. I know this from experience. I am very calm and predictable when I'm worshipping the Lord, but the moment I surrender and that empowering anointing rests upon me, I become very sharp and bold. No one knows what I might do next. You are now responsible for that heavenly empowerment that equips you for ministry.

You feel its anointing tangibly on your physical body. The empowering anointing can come flowing out of you like a river of joy. Psalm 45:1 says, "My heart is inditing a good matter: I speak of the things which I have made touching the king: my tongue is the pen of a ready writer." *Inditing* means boiling up. The psalmist was saying, "My heart is bubbling up or boiling up with a good matter. I can't hold it back. I'm all fired up."

The empowering anointing may come with trembling. In the Old Testament, Daniel felt the anointing on his body, and he began to tremble (Dan. 10:10). This is also something that I experienced in another of Ms. Kuhlman's services. I shook for so long my whole body was trembling. My bones seemed to be coming loose from the joints. I felt that anointing of the Holy Spirit so strong—standing outside and then inside the church she was ministering in in 1973 when I saw her the first time—I was just shaking all over. It looked as if I were cold. But I wasn't cold. I didn't feel cold at all.

The Bible says the prophet Jeremiah felt fire in his mouth (Jer. 5:14) and in his heart (Jer. 20:9). When God spoke through Jeremiah, he felt fire. I have felt that fire. I will never forget preaching at our church, Orlando Christian Center, and in crusades when I felt the fire in my mouth. God puts His fire on your tongue in your mouth. The empowering anointing burns, and you can feel its intensity in your mouth.

Not only is fire in your mouth, but fire is also in your heart. When you preach, you feel it in your bones. You can feel it on your body. I have felt such fire on me, such an inner burning, that I thought, "I'm going to blow up!" Some people's skin gets so red it looks like a tomato. I used to see this with Ms. Kuhlman. She would get so red from the heat of the empowering anointing that you could literally feel it when she came near.

One time when she came near me walking down the aisle, her face was lit up with fire. She was so red—red cheeks, red everything—and when she looked at me, the power of God came upon me. I was knocked out just by her looking at me. I was gone.

There is also a burning in the heart. We learn this from the disciples who met Jesus on the road to Emmaus.

> And they said one to another, Did not our heart burn within
> us, while he talked with us by the way, and while he opened
> to us the scriptures?
>
> —LUKE 24:32

The burning and the fire are two different things. The burning is the same as being constrained, pressed in the Spirit. You burn, and then you testify. It's shut up in you, and everything in you is about to explode. You've got to say it, but the timing may be wrong. You have to wait for the timing of God.

We feel burning many times when God gives us a word of prophecy. But we have to wait for the right moment to release it. If we do not wait for His time, if we give it at the wrong time, it will not affect people as God intended. We must keep quiet until the right time, and then the Word of God will have the greatest impact. Remember:

> The spirits of the prophets are subject to the prophets.
>
> —1 CORINTHIANS 14:32

Fasten your seat belt! We are accelerating into the next demonstration of the empowering anointing.

Chapter 10

THE EMPOWERING ANOINTING CAN BE TRANSFERRED AND STORED

N OW NOT ONLY does the empowering anointing grow, not only do you feel it in your body, but it is also transferrable. You can give it away. In 2 Kings 4:16–29 the Shunammite woman found Elisha and told him her son had died. So Elisha said to his servant Gehazi, "Gird up thy loins, and take my staff in thine hand, go thy way: if thou meet any man, salute him not; and if any salute thee, answer him not again: and lay my staff upon the face of the child" (v. 29).

Nothing happened when Gehazi laid the staff on the boy, because he had been distracted. Elisha had warned him not to talk to anyone because distraction kills the anointing; it shuts down the flow and takes it away from you. Nevertheless, that does not change the fact shown here that the empowering anointing can be transferred to an inanimate object such as this staff.

Another scripture shows the empowering anointing being transferred to a dead body. How else could Elisha's bones raise the Amalekite man in 2 Kings 13? The empowering anointing that remained on the bones of Elisha after he had been buried came in contact with the body of the recently deceased Amalekite man, and that empowering anointing was transferred from Elisha's bones into the second man's dead body, reviving him and bringing him back to life, and the man stood to his feet.

The empowering anointing can be transferred through somebody's hands. Acts 19 says that Paul's hands transferred the Holy Spirit's power. His hands became the channel of power. Through that channel, the empowering anointing was released into pieces of cloth that had been brought, and once the empowering anointing was stored in these remnants, it remained there until it was connected to its purpose.

> And God wrought special miracles by the hands of Paul: so that from his body were brought unto the sick handkerchiefs or aprons, and the diseases departed from them, and the evil spirits went out of them.
>
> —ACTS 19:11–12

I've experienced this in my ministry. Not only is the empowering anointing transferred from my hands when I touch something, but it's also transferred from my body to my shirts and suits. This is the reason I sometimes threw my jacket at people. I have seen more power released when I threw my jacket than when I lay hands. Do you know why? Because my jacket was storing it up.

At first, I couldn't believe it. Then I realized it is like soaking up liquid with a cloth, and as I'm ministering, it keeps absorbing more and more and more and more. Now there's more absorbed into it than I had when I started. It drips into it and saturates it. And the longer I wait, the more power is released.

The empowering anointing builds in an object, on a piece of wood, on cloth. It sometimes drips from clothing. The woman with the issue of blood in Luke 8 understood this. She said, "If

I can just touch Jesus' hem," and the Lord felt the empowering anointing go right through the cloth. "Who touched me?" He asked. He knew power left. He felt it.

I have felt it many times too because it's stored in clothing and other objects. Isn't it amazing that God gives us charge to store it for another time? Think about that.

WE CAN IMPART THIS ANOINTING

The empowering anointing is the only anointing we can impart. I cannot lay hands on anyone and say, "Be saved." Neither can I impart the abiding anointing of 1 John 2:27 that comes at salvation because that is the Lord. I cannot impart the Lord.

I cannot put my hands on someone and say, "Receive the Holy Spirit." That's not even scriptural. But I can impart the *gifts* of the Holy Spirit. Only the Lord Jesus gives the Holy Spirit. (See John 20:22.)

Yet we, the church, can impart the power and anointing of the Holy Spirit. This is the empowering anointing of Acts 1:8. This is the anointing God rubs on you. God applies the empowering anointing on Spirit-filled individuals whom He has entrusted to fill a specific position.

Remember what the Bible says in Acts 6. They had a little situation there. The disciples had multiplied, and the local Jewish believers were not taking care of the believing Hellenistic Jews, who were Greek. Their widows were neglected. So the Greeks came to the apostles to say, "Look, it's not fair what's happening here to us." And here's what the apostle said:

> Wherefore, brethren, look ye out among you seven men of honest report, full of the Holy Ghost and wisdom, whom we may appoint over this business. But we will give ourselves continually to prayer, and to the ministry of the word. And the saying pleased the whole multitude: and they

chose Stephen, a man full of faith and of the Holy Ghost, and Philip, and Prochorus, and Nicanor, and Timon, and Parmenas, and Nicolas a proselyte of Antioch: whom they set before the apostles: and when they had prayed, they laid their hands on them.

—ACTS 6:3–6

Power for ministry came when they laid hands on them. These individuals were filled with the Spirit, born again, faithful, trusted men, and now the apostles laid hands on them and imparted the power for ministry. Before we lay hands on someone, we need to be careful that the Lord has truly told us to do this. (I will share more about that later.) But there are times when God wants us to impart the empowering anointing to others by laying hands on them, and so we must carefully and prayerfully obey Him in this.

THIS ANOINTING AFFECTS OUR WEAKNESS

As I write this, I know that each of us has at least one weakness. When the empowering anointing comes on individuals, it magnifies everything. If your weakness is not under control, the empowering anointing will stir it up because the anointing on you stirs up everything—good and bad. The empowering anointing on you affects your body and soul. It doesn't affect your spirit.

The abiding anointing, the anointing *in* you, affects your spirit and your spiritual life. But the empowering anointing, which is *on* you for ministry, affects your body and soul. It affects your emotions and your physical strength. That's why under the anointing, people get loud. They get bold, aggressive. It's the result of the empowering anointing stirring everything up. It's a good thing because it makes them strong. But it also stirs up the bad stuff—including any weakness in a person's life.

All of us, called and not called, have flaws. I mean everybody; there are no exceptions. All those flaws are stirred under the empowering anointing if they are not properly controlled. The only way you can control your flaws is in the presence of the Lord. When you practice the presence of Jesus, that weakness has nowhere to go. It shrivels up. It's under control. It's still there, but it has no sound, no place. It's as though it's paralyzed, unresponsive. When you minister under the empowering anointing of God, that weakness doesn't show up because the presence of God under the abiding anointing took care of it earlier.

For example, imagine someone who lies a lot. He's always lying about something. He grew up lying because he lived in fear of his dad, mom, or teacher, and he learned to lie his way out of trouble. (All lies begin with fear. If a person is not delivered, the lie becomes a demonic stronghold.) So now he's always lying and can't stop.

But in the presence of God, that lying stronghold loses its power and becomes shriveled. That man always tells the truth when the Lord Jesus is there. He can control the lying because he spends time living in the presence of God, which is the price he must pay to gain this control. The price, I repeat, is spending time with Him. Time with the Lord Jesus is the price that must be paid to gain this control over our weaknesses.

God can now begin to use him because of his faithfulness, and he's been able to control his weakness. If he doesn't spend time in the Word, prayer, and fellowship, then that weakness starts to show up again. (It comes back, and soon it's vigorous and in full bloom once more.) So now he's under the empowering anointing, and he hasn't spent time with the Lord. Next thing you know, he's lying under the empowering anointing, and he lies more when God is using him than when He isn't! Now his biggest lies are told through preaching!

If it's not lying, it's women, pride, greed, or something else. Remember, the empowering anointing magnifies everything in a person—good and bad. People are at their best when God anoints them. However, not only does the best come out, but so does the worst.

This is why the greatest failures happen after the greatest moments of being used by God—regardless of what your ministry is. Your greatest moment is your most dangerous moment because when God uses you, everything is magnified. The majority of ministry leaders who fall into sin do so after their greatest moments.

After a great spiritual victory and a mighty flow of the empowering anointing, our weaknesses can surface and try to overtake us. We must be aware of this sabotage and strengthen ourselves through personal time with the Lord.

It's easy to understand this when you think about what happens after you've spent time ministering. Your emotions are high, but your strength is low. You're physically tired. That's when you are the most vulnerable. If that weakness is stirred up because you did not bring it under control in God's presence before ministering, you can sin right after God uses you.

I heard of a man who could preach with great power, but afterward, he would sleep with a woman he was not married to every time he preached. It bothered me deeply, so I asked Oral Roberts about it. "How can this happen?"

He told me what I've just shared with you: "Everyone is flawed, Benny. The anointing stirs both the good and the bad. Spend time in the presence of God before you minister so that He can shrivel that thing. And pray hard after God uses you, so you don't fall into sin."

That example was about preaching, but it applies to anything you do under the empowering anointing. After you've been used by God, if you find yourself in a situation where your strength is weak, and you know you've got to get alone and pray because that weakness is about to drive you into sin, resist the urge to keep ministering. Stop immediately and walk away, no matter what. If you do not, if you continue to minister in this weakened state, you are draining what little strength you have left, and then you won't be able to pray at all.

I've experienced this when I've been ministering for some time and more people ask me to pray for them, and I think, "Even though I'm tired, I need to be nice. So I've got to pray for them." But I'm telling you that's very dangerous. That's the worst thing you can do when you're tired. Taking time alone in prayer to reconnect with the presence of God after ministering under the empowering anointing is also protection for you. It keeps that weakness whittled down and under control so that your human flaws aren't exposed by your tiredness. So instead, say goodbye and get alone somewhere so you can talk to the Lord Jesus. This way you can remain strong and continue to keep your human nature under His control.

My examples often involved platform ministry, but the empowering anointing in your life will flow through whatever God has called you to do as a Christian. You might be called to a full-time position in a church or large ministry. Perhaps God will use you as an entrepreneur, a business professional, a schoolteacher, a craftsman, an artist, a musician, or a writer. God can use you in your role as a spouse, parent, or grandparent.

Whatever your calling, it is the empowering anointing that enables you to fulfill it. Now let's look at what triggers this outer anointing, because before you can minister *for* the Lord Jesus, you must first minister *to* the Lord Jesus.

THE MYSTERY OF MINISTERING TO THE LORD IN PRAISE

I T'S IMPOSSIBLE TO know the Lord without worship; it is the only thing that reveals Him. Likewise, it is impossible to minister for the Lord without worship; it triggers the power of God and keeps it active and flowing in your life. Both the abiding anointing and the empowering anointing are dependent upon worshipping God. It's an incredible truth, and I'll show this to you in the Scriptures.

> O come, let us sing unto the LORD: let us make a joyful noise to the rock of our salvation. Let us come before His presence with thanksgiving, and make a joyful noise unto him with psalms. For the LORD is a great God, and a great King above all gods. In his hand are the deep places of the earth: the strength of the hills is his also. The sea is his, and he made it: and his hands formed the dry land. O come, let us worship and bow down: let us kneel before the LORD our maker. For he is our God; and we are the people of his pasture, and the sheep of his hand.
>
> —PSALM 95:1–7

This psalm includes some amazing invitations. First, we are invited to sing and make a joyful noise of praise to Him. In that joyful noise there is a revelation of what God has done in our lives. Verse 1 says that He is the "rock of our salvation." Notice the invitation is repeated in verse 2, and it is still connected to praise and thanksgiving. Then the psalmist says He is a great God and a great King, and we are invited to worship Him. Now, I want to focus on this because we must understand how praise differs from worship.

We thank Him because of what He has done in our lives. We praise Him because of His power and His greatness. But it says we *worship* Him for His holiness. Look at verses 6 and 7: "Let us worship and bow down: let us kneel before the LORD our maker. For he is our God; and we are the people of his pasture." Here we see that worship is possible only because we are His people.

We can see from this that thanksgiving and praise are on a different level than worship. We give thanks for what we have seen and experienced; we praise because of what God has done. Praise and thanksgiving are connected to the natural world and our experiences in it. As such, they come from the part of us that is connected to the natural world—our senses and our physical being. But we *worship* from a sense of who He is and how we are connected with Him—through our spirit man. As we worship, we enter into His presence, not merely as beings that He has created but as His children, having the privilege of enjoying His closeness while being intensely aware of His holy nature. It comes from our innermost part, as our spirit man unites with the Spirit of God.

Psalm 96:9 says, "Worship the LORD in the beauty of holiness: fear before him, all the earth." It is not possible to worship God without a revelation of holiness and the fear of the Lord. It is just impossible.

SIX REASONS TO PRAISE

Worshippers cannot worship until they learn to praise. It is a foundational lesson that cannot be overlooked or skipped. I never understood this until I heard Kathryn Kuhlman talk about it. Let's look at six reasons we should praise.

1. Praise is where God lives.

Psalm 22:3 says, "But thou art holy, O thou that inhabitest the praises of Israel." God dwells in our praise. It is where He lives. It's His address. If there is no praise in your daily life, there is no way that you can worship. Without worship you cannot access the fullness of His anointing on your life. Praise is where God lives.

2. Praise gives us access to the throne room of God.

Psalm 100:4 says, "Enter into his gates with thanksgiving, and into his courts with praise." Praise doesn't bring us into the throne room; it only opens the door to the throne room. Only worship allows us to draw near to the throne of God, but praise makes the way open. When you praise the Lord, you will be invited to come closer. It gives you access.

3. Praise changes the atmosphere in and around our lives.

Isaiah 61:3–4 says, "To appoint unto them that mourn in Zion, to give unto them beauty for ashes, the oil of joy for mourning, the garment of praise for the spirit of heaviness; that they might be called trees of righteousness, the planting of the LORD, that he might be glorified. And they shall build the old wastes, they shall raise up the former desolations, and they shall repair the waste cities, the desolations of many generations." Think about the *repair* that comes when you praise the Lord. Putting on a new garment isn't just about feeling better. It's about starting to live righteously with power. It is about God beginning to use you to repair all the damage that the enemy has done in your life and in others.

4. Praise brings deliverance.

Psalm 50:23 says, "Whoso offereth praise glorifieth me: and to him that ordereth his conversation aright will I shew the salvation of God." That means deliverance. If you are going through a demonic attack, praise has great power to deliver you. If there's trouble, begin to praise Him. As the praise of God takes over the space around you, the trouble you have been experiencing will be forced to its knees and it must leave.

Praise has a sound. It is not just the sound of voices raised or a crowd clapping. Praise sounds like crashing chains. Ask Paul and Silas. When we praise God in our prison, chains crash to the floor and prison doors swing open. Our praise even has power to set others free. When Paul and Silas praised, it was so powerful that it shook the prison. The spiritual affected the natural.

> And at midnight Paul and Silas prayed, and sang praises unto God: and the prisoners heard them. And suddenly there was a great earthquake, so that the foundations of the prison were shaken: and immediately all the doors were opened, and every one's bands were loosed.
>
> —ACTS 16:25–26

Even the keeper of the prison and his whole household were saved and baptized as a result of Paul and Silas and their praise. Praise sets people free!

5. Praise brings protection and preservation to your life.

Psalm 59:17 says, "Unto thee, O my strength, will I sing: for God is my defence, and the God of my mercy." David was praising the Lord for being his defense, which is protection. Then in Psalm 71:6–7, he talks about preservation: "By thee have I been holden up from the womb: thou art he that took me out of my mother's bowels: my praise shall be continually of thee. I am as a wonder unto many; but thou art my strong refuge." Both protection and preservation are found under the covering of praise.

6. Praise is our weapon of war.

Psalm 149:6, 8–9 says, "Let the high praises of God be in their mouth, and a two-edged sword in their hand...to bind their kings with chains, and their nobles with fetters of iron; to execute upon them the judgment written: this honour have all his saints. Praise ye the LORD." In praise we find the power to carry out God's judgment against our enemies. In David's time this meant physically restraining men who were in power and removing them from their thrones. In our time, however, we are not battling against men, as David was. Ephesians 6:12 tells us that "we wrestle not against flesh and blood, but against principalities, against powers, against the rulers of the darkness of this world, against spiritual wickedness in high places." We use praise to take down these spiritual enemies, not to conquer other people. When we lift our voices in praise, we disarm these spiritual powers. Once we have done so, even people who have operated under the wicked influence of demonic powers will be disarmed and lose what power they had.

These lessons from God's precious Word tell us what happens when we praise the Lord: It's where God lives; it gives us access; it changes our garments; it brings us deliverance, protection, and preservation; it's our weapon of war. Praise releases the power of God to do battle on our behalf. In praise we find what we lacked. In praise, victory is ours!

Chapter 12

WHEN PRAISE TURNS TO WORSHIP

W E CANNOT WORSHIP until we have entered in through praise. Psalm 100:4 says we "enter into his gates with thanksgiving, and into his courts with praise." Praise erupts in the courts and brings us to the doorway. As we enter, our thanksgiving and praise lead us into worship.

Now Psalm 48:1 provides another insight on how we are to enter. It says, "Great is the LORD, and *greatly* to be praised." This verse says something powerful: God will not accept half-hearted praise. What the Scripture is saying is, "He's so great—how dare you praise Him with half a heart? He won't accept that." This verse tells us how we are to enter: praising and thanking Him with full hearts, not half hearts. He didn't halfway save us. He didn't halfway redeem us. We must never insult Him by praising Him halfway. If we return to Psalm 95:3–5, we see why we have to praise God with our whole hearts.

> For the LORD is a great God, and a great King above all gods. In his hand are the deep places of the earth: the strength of the hills is his also. The sea is his, and he made it: and his hands formed the dry land.

I once traveled to Sinai, and I will never forget the experience of climbing Mount Sinai at night. Because there was no pollution, we could clearly see the Milky Way. At the sight of it we broke into spontaneous, exuberant praise like never before. Everything in us erupted, and we began shouting our praises with tears flowing down our cheeks. We realized God's greatness because we saw the Milky Way. Isaiah 40:12 says God marked off the heavens with the span of His hand. God created the stars of the midnight sky. Scripture declares God counts the stars and gives them names. Oh, what a mighty God we serve!

Nature reveals His greatness to us, but only the Holy Spirit can reveal His holiness. When you see His holiness, your attitude toward Him and the way you interact with Him will completely change. You will fall on your face and worship the Lord. This depth of worship will transform your life.

Let me discuss an important reason for this shift from praise to worship. Praise crucifies the flesh, and worship puts a new robe on us. As you dismantle the influence of your flesh through praise, it falls into submission to Him. Now as you dress yourself in the robe of worship, you invite God's presence in a new way.

You can see how this process progresses. First, you destroy the weaknesses of your flesh with the praise; then you pick up the robe of worship and put it on. When you add the deeper level of worship to your praise, you elevate yourself into a closer encounter with the presence of God.

We see this shift from praise to worship once again in David's call to worship.

> O come, let us worship and bow down: let us kneel before the LORD our maker. For he is our God; and we are the people of his pasture, and the sheep of his hand. To day if ye will hear his voice...
>
> —PSALM 95:6–7

These verses show how our experience changes as our worship brings us to the heart of the matter. We enter quietness in verse 6: "O come, let us worship and bow down: let us kneel before the LORD our maker." When we bow down, we are not screaming or shouting. We are peaceful and reverent as we allow worship to lower us into submission before the greatness of our God.

Then, verse 7 says, "To day if ye will hear his voice." This implies that your voice is quiet so that you can hear His. You are in a place of quietness when you are worshipping. Verse 7 gives two reasons to be quiet: (1) He is our God, and (2) we are the people of His pasture, meaning we are under His care.

He is our God. He is the only Being worthy of worship. You may be permitted to praise a person, but you are not allowed to *worship* a person. You may only worship God. One reason is that whatever you worship will control you.

Many people worship other people, and they come under bondage. They are controlled by an individual they have thought of too highly. They placed that person on a pedestal, but soon everything came crashing down.

If we do not worship the Lord, then is He really our God? Is He really our Lord? Remember what the Lord Jesus says in Matthew 7, and I'm paraphrasing: "You call me Lord, but you don't live it." How does this happen to people? They stop living it because they stop worshipping Him as Lord. Worship is the key.

We worship because we are responding to His love, His care. Psalm 95:7 says, "We are the people of his pasture, and the sheep of his hand." That shows that we are in His care, and we worship in response to receiving that care.

Amazingly the psalm doesn't end here; it closes with a warning. Verses 8–11 say,

> Harden not your heart, as in the provocation, and as in
> the day of temptation in the wilderness: when your fathers

tempted me, proved me, and saw my work. Forty years long was I grieved with this generation, and said, It is a people that do err in their heart, and they have not known my ways: Unto whom I sware in my wrath that they should not enter into my rest.

Worship brings us into faith, and faith brings us into rest. But what is His rest? Rest means no more striving. You do not have to work to achieve His rest; you just have to receive it. He has done it all, so enter in and rest. The Christian life is not all "do, do, do." The Lord Jesus didn't say, "Do," on the cross. He said, "Done."

Now, this brings a decision before us: Do we worship or not? When we worship, we hear His voice. Upon hearing His voice, we obey and enter His rest. So worship brings us into rest. Jeremiah talked about this too.

But this thing commanded I them, saying, Obey my voice, and I will be your God, and ye shall be my people: and walk ye in all the ways that I have commanded you, that it may be well unto you.

—JEREMIAH 7:23

If it is well with you, you are in a place of blessings and rest. It's not about prayer and fasting, begging and pleading, pounding the floor, and concluding that God is not listening to you. You are not trying to make it happen; it is happening by itself. Again, obedience follows worship. Worship produces obedience. Praise does not produce obedience; worship does. You see, the moment you move from praise into worship, you hear His voice. Once you obey His voice, there is rest.

Nothing moves the hand of God as quickly as worship—nothing.

Back in the 1970s I would lie on my bed and worship God deep in the night. Those were wonderful hours for me! God began to visit me in those early days because I spent time worshipping Him. I played Bill Gaither's *Alleluia!* album over and over again. I would lie on my bed with my hands up as my tears soaked my pillow, just playing those worship songs with the lights off. I would talk to the Lord Jesus and love Him. I believe that this intimacy with the Lord is what launched my ministry. Every time I reach this level of intimacy again, I see a new resurrection of the anointing in my meetings.

Worship is vital. People who don't worship are dry and dead. And when they try to minister, it is obvious there is no anointing there. You just want it to *stop* because it is powerless. But when true worshippers minister, the atmosphere becomes charged with dynamic power. The presence of God cannot be mistaken here. Everyone is glued to every single thing that these worshippers say and do because God is there with them. When praise turns to worship, everything changes. The climate shifts and lives are transformed. You can sense His presence best in an atmosphere of worship.

Chapter 13

MINISTRY *TO* THE LORD, NOT *FOR* THE LORD

E VERYTHING I'VE BEEN writing about in these past two chapters is what I call ministering to the Lord. When you spend time worshipping and loving the Lord, you minister *to* the Lord, not *for* the Lord. Your ministry *to* the Lord is the foundation of your ministry *for* the Lord. This is a compelling truth. Let it soak into your very being.

Your ministry to the Lord is the foundation of your ministry for the Lord.

Deuteronomy 10:8 talks about God establishing the Levitical order:

> At that time the LORD separated the tribe of Levi, to bear the ark of the covenant of the LORD, to stand before the LORD to minister unto him, and to bless in his name, unto this day.

God established a whole tribe assigned to do one thing only: minister to the Lord. They were to stand before the Lord to minister unto Him.

Our ministry *to* God comes before our ministry *for* God. You cannot minister to people if you have not ministered to Him first, because you can't give away what you don't have. If you've been in His presence, you can take people there. If you've been in His presence, you know exactly how to get in and take them with you. When you worship, He shows up.

Churches everywhere have talented singers as their worship leaders who often don't spend enough time with the Lord. They cannot lead the congregation to a place in the presence of the Lord if they seldom spend time there. If we want a deeper experience in the presence of God in our churches and in our ministries, then we must check our priorities and embrace the power of personal communion with the Lord and our ministry *to* the Lord so we can have a dynamic ministry *for* the Lord. We need to encourage our worship leaders and ministers on the importance of having a personal daily walk with the Lord Jesus. It is absolutely imperative that our leaders actively lead by example in this area, demonstrating a daily time of personal worship.

When I held crusades, I would worship from 2:00 p.m. to service time. I focused on the Lord for several hours. Then I'd walk on that platform, and He walked on with me. Why? He'd been with me since 2:00 p.m. I realize you likely have a very different calling than mine. Nonetheless, you must spend enough time with the Lord to keep your spiritual life strong and vibrant.

In 1 Samuel 3:1 Scripture says that Israel was going through spiritual dryness, a season of spiritual famine. The voice of the Lord was not heard. It says, "And the child Samuel ministered unto the LORD before Eli. And the word of the LORD was precious in those days; there was no open vision." One can't help but notice that this is the condition of America and the world now.

Samuel started ministering to the Lord when he was a child, which brought back the prophetic. When Samuel lay down, the Lord called his name. He did not even recognize the voice of the Lord the first, second, or third time. Then, the fourth time, he realized it was the Lord speaking. But why did God speak to him? Because he was ministering to the Lord. It goes back to what I wrote about Psalm 95. When you start worshipping, God will talk to you. It's quite simple. He even spoke to a little boy who had never heard His voice before.

Revival came to Israel because one little boy changed the whole atmosphere by ministering to God. What would happen to Canada, the United States, Kenya, and China if God's children began ministering to Him? Revival would be poured out upon our nations. If God heard Samuel, He will hear you. If God poured out revival for Israel, He will do it for *your* nation. Think what you can do if you begin to minister to the Lord and spend more time worshipping than begging, more time worshipping than fasting, more time worshipping than praying.

In 1 Samuel 3 God visited Israel because of a little boy, and in 2 Chronicles 5:13 Solomon finished building the temple. God didn't show up when they finished the building. He didn't show up when they sacrificed all the animals. He showed up when all the people of Israel worshipped the Lord in one voice. The glory of God descended. In 2 Chronicles 7:1–3 the fire also fell on Israel because they ministered to the Lord.

In Acts 13 God called the apostle Paul while he ministered to the Lord. Verse 2 says, "As they ministered to the LORD, and fasted, the Holy Ghost said, Separate me Barnabas and Saul [who became known as Paul] for the work whereunto I have called them." God did not call Paul on the road to Damascus. God didn't call him when he went to Arabia either. Paul went to Arabia for fourteen years and then came to Jerusalem to ensure that what he had heard and seen was true. He went back into tent making in his hometown.

Barnabas found him and brought him to Antioch, which is present-day Syria. While he was in Antioch ministering to the

Lord, God said, "Now I want him." They were ministering to the Lord. Every time worship moves, God moves, calling people into ministry like Paul.

Do you want God to call you into ministry? Do you want to be used of God? Today, begin to minister *to* God; make it your priority. The practice of your ministry *to* the Lord will be the foundation, the launching pad of your ministry *for* the Lord.

In Daniel 7 angels minister to the Lord, and as a result, judgment falls on the wicked. The Antichrist is judged because of worship. It's all there.

> I beheld till the thrones were cast down, and the Ancient of days did sit, whose garment was white as snow, and the hair of his head like the pure wool: his throne was like the fiery flame, and his wheels as burning fire. A fiery stream issued and came forth from before him: thousand thousands ministered unto him, and ten thousand times ten thousand stood before him: the judgment was set, and the books were opened. I beheld then because of the voice of the great words which the horn spake: I beheld even till the beast was slain, and his body destroyed, and given to the burning flame.
>
> —Daniel 7:9–11

God destroys the Antichrist as a result of worship in glory. It moves the hand of God against His enemies. When you are a worshipper, you do not have to fight your enemies. God will take care of it for you; His army is sent to battle on your behalf. Worshippers are protected. God will fight for you.

God Sets His Love Upon Us

Now I want to focus on why we have such power with God. It is because we are His people. We are His children. Deuteronomy

32:9 says, "The LORD's portion is his people." Deuteronomy 7:7 says that He sets His love upon us. God did not set His love on the angels. He set His love upon us, and the Bible very clearly says in 1 John 4:19 that He loved us before we loved Him:

> We love him, because he first loved us.

We are the church of Jesus Christ; we are God's children. He loves us with unconditional and eternal love. As His beloved children, we have so much influence with Him. When we pray, we spend too much of our time focused on our problems, our needs, our enemies, and our spiritual battles. This precious time would be better spent in expressing our love, devotion, and worship to the One who can transform our lives and work every situation for our good.

Two verses in Isaiah 43 say something powerful. In verse 7 God declares that He created you for Himself. In verse 21 He restates that.

> Even every one that is called by my name; for I have created him for my glory, I have formed him; yea, I have made him.... This people have I formed for myself; they shall show forth my praise.
>
> —ISAIAH 43:7, 21

Why did He create you? That you might worship the Lord. This is the purpose for which we were created; everything that we are called to do leads back to this singular purpose. *We were created to worship Him.* That's very, very powerful.

In Ephesians we see that when we give ourselves to Him, He gives Himself to us.

> Cease not to give thanks for you, making mention of you in my prayers; that the God of our Lord Jesus Christ, the

> Father of glory, may give unto you the spirit of wisdom and
> revelation in the knowledge of him: the eyes of your under-
> standing being enlightened; that ye may know what is the
> hope of his calling, and what the riches of the glory of his
> inheritance in the saints.
>
> —EPHESIANS 1:16–18

He wants to pour His riches into you. God's purpose in saving you is so that you can know Him. The hope of His calling is the riches of the glory of His inheritance in the saints. Think about that one. There's an inheritance *in* you. He gives you Himself as you give Him yourself.

Moses didn't just nod his head toward God in acknowledgement; he threw himself to the ground and worshipped.

> Moses immediately threw himself to the ground and
> worshiped.
>
> —EXODUS 34:8, NLT

One worshipping man saved an entire nation. Never underestimate the power that is unleashed when we worship God.

Do you remember the demon-possessed child of the woman in Matthew 15:21–28? She went to the Lord, and He ignored her. The disciples tried to get rid of her, so she went back to Jesus. He called her an outsider, one outside the covenant at the time, but she fell down and worshipped Him. When she did that, she broke through everything that was in her way.

At that time, only Israel was entitled to receive anything from God. This woman had no right to expect anything from Jesus, but she didn't let that stop her.

> Then Jesus went thence, and departed into the coasts of
> Tyre and Sidon [northern Israel and southern Lebanon].
> And, behold, a woman of Canaan came out of the same

coasts, and cried unto him, saying, Have mercy on me, O Lord, thou son of David; my daughter is grievously vexed with a devil. But he answered her not a word. And his disciples came and besought him, saying, Send her away; for she crieth after us. But he answered and said, I am not sent but unto the lost sheep of the house of Israel. Then came she and worshipped him, saying, Lord, help me.

—MATTHEW 15:21–25

Her worship changed everything. Before she worshipped, Jesus ignored her very existence. After she worshipped, the Lord addressed her for the first time. He didn't give her the answer she wanted, but she still kept worshipping Him, and her worship broke through.

Then Jesus answered and said unto her, O woman, great is thy faith; be it unto thee even as thou wilt. And her daughter was made whole from that very hour.

—MATTHEW 15:28

"Great is your faith," He told her. "Let it be done even as you will." So she canceled the opposition with worship, and her daughter was healed.

Let's take another look at Paul and Silas in prison in Acts 16.

And at midnight Paul and Silas prayed, and sang praises unto God: and the prisoners heard them. And suddenly there was a great earthquake, so that the foundations of the prison were shaken: and immediately all the doors were opened, and every one's bands were loosed.

—ACTS 16:25–26

When they started worshipping, the jail doors opened and their chains came loose. God still moves the same way He did back then.

That is the key to power. When you worship the Lord wherever you are, God will show up and change your life. Worship will never wear you out. Other things may weary you, but worship will not.

Before Billy Graham died, he reportedly was asked, "What would you have done differently?" He said, "I would have stayed home more and told Jesus how much I love Him."

I live for one thing: to give all the glory to the Lord Jesus. I do this by honoring His precious name, loving Him with all my being, and being pleasing to Him. When I look back on my life, I want to be able to say that I did these things. It's that simple.

After you put this book down today, you might find yourself unable to sleep. Put on some worship music and talk to the Lord while you're lying down. I promise you that if you make time for Him, He will meet you there. And you will wake up feeling refreshed and strong because the Lord visited you.

Chapter 14

THE MYSTERY OF SIPHONING THE ANOINTING

THE LAST SERVICE Kathryn Kuhlman ever preached in Pittsburgh, Pennsylvania, was a tough one for her. I know because I was there.

I attended that day as I had many of her services before. Afterward I made arrangements through her staff to meet her two weeks later. Sadly, two weeks later she was not able to be there because she was dying. And I went home very disappointed that I would never meet Kathryn Kuhlman.

A year later, to my utter shock Maggie Hartner, who ran the Kathryn Kuhlman Foundation, told me that I would conduct Ms. Kuhlman's memorial service in Pittsburgh. I had begun preaching as an evangelist by then, but I was only twenty-four years old, and I had never even met her. How could I be the one who was supposed to conduct the memorial service? I was so scared I didn't even want to ask her why they had chosen me. But I was thinking, "Why me? Why didn't you choose someone else who knew her?" I couldn't understand it, but I took it as a great honor and did my best to prepare.

The day of the service arrived. That afternoon, I went to the foundation's beautiful office on the seventh floor of the Carlton hotel in downtown Pittsburgh. I walked in and saw pictures of John F. Kennedy hanging on the walls alongside beautiful artwork. I met Maggie Hartner, and she showed me Ms. Kuhlman's chair. I was so in awe of her that I didn't even want to go near it. I was like a kid in a candy store, looking around in amazement.

As I spoke with Maggie, she brought up that I would be preaching the service later that day, and then she made this statement: "Benny, don't you go off and pray and beg God to anoint you. You'll get so tied up in yourself that God won't be able to use you." She told me to take a nap instead. I couldn't believe it!

Since then I have learned a lot about the anointing from that statement. But at the time, I was thinking, "This is the most unspiritual woman I have ever met! I am not going to take a nap. I don't care what she says!" So I did exactly what she told me not to do: I went and begged, "Oh, God! Oh, Jesus!" I was so scared that I got all tied up.

Then the service time came. I looked out from behind the curtain, and I got even more scared. I saw the big crowd in Carnegie Music Hall, one of the most beautiful buildings in Pittsburgh. All the people who had worked with Ms. Kuhlman were there, and the choir was in the choir loft. And little Benny Hinn was supposed to minister? Nobody knew who Benny Hinn was. Nobody even knew what I looked like.

It was time to get started. Jimmie McDonald, Ms. Kuhlman's soloist, was to open the service by showing the only film of her ministry that she ever allowed to be made. It was from Las Vegas and recorded her last service held in a big stadium.

The plan was that Jimmie McDonald would introduce me before the film, which would last ninety minutes, and then, when the film was over, he would sing, "There's Something About That Name." Then, as he sang, I was supposed to walk out on the stage and take it from there.

They showed the film, and I waited behind the curtain.

The film ended, and he sang the song. I was still behind the curtain.

He sang it a second time. I was still behind the curtain.

Then Jimmie McDonald said to the crowd, "Now as we sing it for the last time, Benny Hinn will walk on," and he sang it again. When they finished, I was still behind the curtain!

I remained glued to my spot until an usher came up behind me and forced me out on the platform! That was my introduction to the Kathryn Kuhlman crowd.

The musicians continued to play softly and started playing something else. Now, because I was so scared, my brain froze, and all I could do was sing the same song again. But because the musicians had started playing something else, they were in another key. I started singing in that key, and it was so high that I sang it terribly. The musicians did not know how to follow me, so they stopped, and I found myself singing it a cappella.

About halfway through I just stopped. I could not continue singing because it was so high. The crowd was staring at me, and I was thinking about how much I wanted to run off the stage and go home. Then something happened that I'll never forget.

Everybody was still standing, and they were all looking at me. It was a total disaster until I threw up my hands and cried, "Dear Jesus, Dear Jesus! I cannot do it! I cannot do it!"

And I heard the Lord say, "I'm glad! Now I will!"

As I began ministering, the Lord took over, and the power of God descended mightily. People began to get healed. The ladies who had ministered with Ms. Kuhlman came out of their seats and ran down the aisle. People began coming out of wheelchairs. The miracle-working power of God descended. I was completely amazed, and so was the Kathryn Kuhlman staff. When they saw what happened, Maggie came up to me and said, "Kiddo, you've got it." I did not know what she meant by that. Then she said, "We want you to come back monthly. So I went monthly and began holding services for the Kathryn Kuhlman Foundation at Soldiers and Sailors Memorial Auditorium, and later I began to travel with the foundation all over the United States and Canada. I did that for four years, and that is when people began to know about the ministry that the Lord had given me.

It all started when I said, "I cannot do it!" The problem with too many Christians and ministry leaders is that they think they can do it. I have news for you: *You cannot do it.* Only God can! You have to surrender. Don't try to figure it out.

After the memorial service, Maggie came up to me and said, "Kathryn always said, 'It's not your prayers; it's not your ability; it's your surrender.' Learn how to surrender, Benny." I knew her words held the key to ministering under the powerful anointing of God, so I went back to my hotel room and began praying for the Lord to teach me how to surrender.

SURRENDER IS THE SIPHON

I shared that story about surrender for a reason. It is the key to ministering under the empowering anointing. When the Lord and you become one at salvation, the abiding anointing is immediately released in you. This anointing produces hunger, faith, and love for the Lord. It ignites the Word, fellowship, and worship. Then, as God begins to transform you, the empowering anointing *for ministry* descends on you. The abiding anointing is working, and it brings clarity to the empowering anointing for ministry. There's nothing you can do to make the empowering anointing descend, but once it does, you are the one who has to release it. I refer to this release as siphoning the anointing.

This truth about siphoning is found in Deuteronomy 32:13. I will go into more detail in the next chapter.

Now, if you miss this next point, you'll miss a lot, so focus on these words: *surrender is the siphon.* In other words, you siphon the anointing when you surrender to the presence of the Lord. If everyone would learn how to do this, no one would ever lack the power of God.

Surrender is the siphon.

That's why the power of God descended when I surrendered in Kathryn Kuhlman's memorial service. In the moment of my surrender the Lord Jesus came and touched His people. I went to the hotel that night and began praying for the Lord to teach me to surrender, and I learned this lesson. It's why I worship in all my meetings to this day. Anytime I lead people to believe God for healing and miracles, we worship the Lord. As we worship God, there comes the point where the Lord Jesus becomes very real. And when Jesus becomes real to me, I surrender. The minute I surrender, the power descends. It's like a blanket that covers my being.

I believe God wants to use you in the last days, which are coming. But you have to learn how to siphon the anointing out of God's glory and presence. The key is surrendering at that moment when Jesus becomes real to you. Why? You cannot surrender to One you don't know. You cannot surrender to One who is not real to you. You are not surrendering to air; you are surrendering to a person. That's why you can only surrender when He makes Himself tangible to you.

Chapter 15

THE MYSTERY OF THE HIGH PLACES

T HE HIGH PLACES are where we meet the Lord face to face. To understand this from the Word of God, let's read the following scripture about Jacob.

> He made him ride on the high places of the earth, that he might eat the increase of the fields; and he made him to suck honey out of the rock, and oil out of the flinty rock.
> —DEUTERONOMY 32:13

The "high places of the earth" are places where the empowering anointing and the Word of God flow freely. They are places of intense worship. Isaiah talks about the high places when he talks about where the eagle can soar. Isaiah says, "They that wait upon the LORD shall renew their strength; they shall mount up" (Isa. 40:31). Notice it doesn't say they'll go down; it says up. Psalm 91 refers to it too: the secret place of the Most High is the high place. It's the same place. So high places of the earth are places where the demonic cannot function.

Take another look at Deuteronomy 32:13. When it says, "He made him ride on the high places of the earth," worship brings you there. When Moses says, "That he might eat the increase of the fields," that's the Word coming alive again in you, producing more worship and transformation.

When Moses says, "And he made him to suck [or siphon] honey out of the rock," the rock is the Lord. It's saying as you surrender, He pours out more of His Word into your being and His oil onto your being.

Look at the order. The oil is flowing because of the honey. Honey is first, then oil. The increase of the field is first, then the anointing. You receive the Word, and it ignites worship, which ignites transformation. (Then the empowering anointing comes upon you for ministry, and you siphon it right out by surrendering to the Lord.)

You have to experience the high places of the spirit to have the empowering anointing for ministry. God gives it to you, but you will not receive it if you do not know how to siphon it. The high places are where God's tangible reality is known. When you are deep in the Word, communion, and worship, you rise in the spirit to a high plateau. I want to put it another way to make sure you grasp this. When you worship, and the Word of God and communion are deep, your spirit man goes to a high place. And in that high place, the presence of God is tangible. It goes beyond being felt; it is *known*.

When the presence of the Lord Jesus is real, the soul will be stilled, just as I discussed in chapter 7. "Be still, and know that I am God" (Ps. 46:10). At the moment the Lord becomes real, everything becomes quiet. In the presence of the Lord tears are the language. In the presence of the Lord there's such reality that it disconnects the flesh. In other words, when the presence of the Lord is real, you reach a point where you lose sight of yourself. God's presence will overtake your presence. When God's presence overtakes your presence, you're in the high place. When you lose sight of yourself, that's when you can siphon the anointing.

And it came to pass, when Moses came down from mount
Sinai with the two tables of testimony in Moses' hand, when
he came down from the mount, that Moses wist not that
the skin of his face shone while he talked with him.

—EXODUS 34:29

Let's get back to Deuteronomy 32:13, which speaks of increased
fields, honey, and oil. This means the high places are a place of
great spiritual abundance. When you are in worship, when you
are in those lovely places where the presence of Jesus is more real
than your own life, there are abundant blessings. Everything is
abundant in those places.

Remember, waiting upon the Lord is the key. If you aren't
willing to wait, you will never get there. But once you're there,
you're in amazing abundance. That's where the honey starts to
flow out of the rock, representing the revelation truth of the
Word. That's when God begins to reveal His Word to you, and
now it's easy to surrender to the Word of God because you're in
the high place. The empowering anointing is flowing, so it is not
hard labor.

THREE AVENUES TO THE HIGH PLACE

You can get to the high place all by yourself. You don't have to
lead a large crowd in an auditorium like I often describe; you
don't need anyone else with you. There are three avenues to
the high place. The Word of God is the first avenue, fellowship
(prayer) is the second avenue, and worship is the third avenue to
the high place.

Does the order matter? I believe it does. The Word fuels your
fellowship with God in prayer. When you read the Word, not
only does He quicken your fellowship with Him; He ignites it!
Prayer, which I call fellowship because that's what it is, can bring

you to the high place. But fellowship is ignited and energized by the Word. Fellowship without the Word has no power.

As you spend time in God's precious Word, it begins to bring life-giving power to your soul and spirit. The Word of God is living, and it will instantly birth fellowship with God. You step into incredible fellowship with the Lord. You tell Him how much you love Him and how glorious He is.

You connect with the Lord's heart, and then worship comes out of that. And when worship begins, it accelerates your speed. You go from low to high levels—to the high place—and you're moving quickly. When you get up there, everything is abundant and free.

Then the anointing is revealed. You say, "Pastor Benny, why do you say it's revealed?" The Bible says God's power is hidden.

> And his brightness was as the light; he had horns coming out of his hand: *and there was the hiding of his power.*
> —HABAKKUK 3:4

You see, Habakkuk 3:4 and Deuteronomy 32:13 go together. When His hidden power is revealed, when the anointing is ready to be released, you have to siphon it. And again, how do you siphon that anointing? You surrender.

When I minister before a crowd, and I'm worshipping in the high place, that's when I sing the song "Alleluia" because it enables the crowd to enter into the presence of God. When I'm in that high place of worship and sing that song, I know that it brings His reality, substance, and tangibility to me. When the Lord becomes real to me, I surrender.

If you don't have a public ministry like mine, your private worship of the Lord can take you to the high place. When you are in that place, you surrender so easily. There's no struggle with it. You don't have to work at it. You move right into the empowering anointing, and then you feel God's power on your body. Now His power flows through you to accomplish whatever Christian service He has called you to do.

Chapter 16

THE MYSTERY OF THE ELIJAH
FLOW AND THE ELISHA FLOW

W
HAT HAPPENS AFTER you have siphoned the anointing with your surrender? To answer that, I must explain the Elijah flow and the Elisha flow. Simply put, the Elijah flow is the declaration of the Word of God, and the Elisha flow is worship in the presence of the Lord.

Worship in the ministry of Elisha brought the manifestation of the Spirit of the Lord to him. But the preaching of Elijah brought the manifestation of God's Word to him. Elijah's preaching brought him into the flow of the anointing for ministry. For Elisha it was worship.

The moment you preach the Word and this manifests the presence of Jesus, you must surrender. The moment your worship manifests the presence of Jesus, you must surrender. *If you keep preaching or worshipping, you lose it.* The minute the Lord manifests, He's saying to you, "I'm ready to touch My people. Let Me." You brought Him on the scene with your preaching or worship. Now you must release the Lord's presence and power by your surrender.

If you don't surrender, you've just lost that moment, and it may not come that way again. You may have to worship for a

109

long time to rebuild almost from ground zero. It's a lot of work. Never allow anyone to interfere with that moment of worship, no matter how important they are to you.

The minute the presence of the Lord manifests, you must surrender. You may be teaching, preaching, leading a Bible study or small group, or ministering to an individual, and you think you have much more to say, but the presence of the Lord manifests. Stop talking right then and surrender to Him.

Don't let your message ruin the moment for the people or the person you are ministering to. You brought the Lord's presence with the Word, and you may say to yourself, "Well, I'm not done yet." But when God says to you, "You are done. I'm here," you must immediately surrender. After you surrender, the Lord begins flowing. The Lord is moving. You've siphoned His power through surrender.

When He manifests His presence to you, you must surrender. You surrender to the Person of Christ Jesus. Once He becomes real through the Word or through worship, you have to surrender. There are times when you might need to go another step and quietly pray in tongues on your own.

Here is another important point: the people you minister to cannot join you in surrendering to the Lord. Only you can siphon the anointing; they cannot. It's *your* worship. It's *your* preaching or teaching. It's not their worship. You are the transmitter; they are the receivers. It's the worship of the transmitter that moves God, not the worship of the receivers. As you are worshipping, they join you. As they join you, the Lord ministers to them also.

This brings something to my mind: I've known some ministers, and I'm sure some people, who might feel somehow unworthy to worship God publicly. You must settle in your heart now: worship is not about the worthiness of the worshipper. *Worship is about the worthiness of the One being worshipped.* God is worthy of our worship!

The crowd's worship is still vital in a platform ministry setting because it connects them to your surrender. When you surrender, their worship immediately manifests the presence of the Lord Jesus to them. Their worship immediately brings His reality to them. The reality of the Lord will first touch you, the servant, and then it will touch the people who are there to receive ministry.

Whether you are worshipping God alone or publicly, use songs that have proved themselves to move Him. I love songs such as "Alleluia," "Glory to the Lamb," and "Oh, the Glory of His Presence." Why? Those songs were written out of an experience with the Lord, so they bring the experience with the Lord back. I'm not saying those are the only anointed songs. But if you choose a song that's not anointed, you will lose because there's no touch upon it.

I don't think I ever heard Kathryn Kuhlman sing more than a handful of songs: "How Great Thou Art," "He Touched Me," "He's the Savior of My Soul," which she wrote, "There's Something About That Name," and always "Alleluia." The glory would fall because these were songs that touched her heart. They became her own, and when she sang them, her worship touched the Lord's heart. He manifested to her. He became real to her.

She surrendered to Him, and as a result of her surrender, the presence of God permeated the auditorium. As the presence of God began to permeate the auditorium, the people sensed His presence as they worshipped Him, and that's when miracles take place. That's when that mighty power touches them.

When I surrender, which has happened thousands of times now, I immediately feel the power descend on me. I have felt electricity. I have felt fire. I have felt the overpowering anointing of the Lord. Sometimes it was such glorious power that I felt like my flesh was going to blow up. At that moment, I become bold, strong, demonstrative, loud, and intense because it's emotional.

When the power of God starts to flow through your physical body, your skin starts to feel it. Your entire body is under it. It starts to drip into your clothing. The power is now ready to flow to the people God wants to touch through you.

The needs of the people and their hunger for the Lord calls out to the empowering anointing that is upon you. When they unite with the Lord's presence and surrender, the power descends on them, and they're healed. The reality of His presence meets their needs, fills their hunger, and changes their lives.

I often find that people are not able to receive what the Lord wants to give them if they're all tied up with themselves. They have to let go. If they focus on themselves or their sickness or whatever problem they may face, they're not focusing on the Lord. I've often said, when the Lord Jesus becomes more real than the sickness, that sickness will go immediately. His reality will force out that sickness.

No matter where you are ministering, things may happen that cause the empowering anointing to weaken: people moving around, someone talking, a strange sound. Many things can cause distractions that lessen or weaken the empowering anointing if you allow it. When you are ministering to someone one-on-one and that happens, if the setting is appropriate, you can begin worshipping right there because worship will cause the empowering anointing to descend again. You can also read the Word and pray in tongues if needed. If the setting doesn't allow this, you can simply pray for that person and then move on.

If you are ministering in a public meeting and the empowering anointing weakens, you can begin worshipping or preaching the Word. Sometimes you have already ministered the Word, you already led the people in worship, and you yourself have worshipped, but you feel you have not yet reached the high place that He wants you to attain. In those cases, it is as if the Lord is telling you to pray a little longer. That's when you need to pray in tongues.

Let me quickly mention a few things about praying in tongues to yourself and quietly.

- Prayer in tongues by itself will not bring the anointing. It must happen after preaching the Word or worship, after you've built a pathway into the realm of the spirit.

- Praying in tongues is not always needed. In one out of three meetings, I feel I need to go further by speaking in tongues. Other times, the presence of God will descend without tongues having been used. Listen to the voice of the Lord, then obey.

- The need for tongues depends on the spiritual atmosphere around you. In the crusades, I rarely prayed in tongues publicly. When I minister in churches or conferences and the expectation or faith is not high, praying in tongues can create an atmosphere of faith. Tongues may be needed if things are in your head that shouldn't be there. You have got to be clear from them. We'll discuss this more at a later point.

No matter how God uses you, when the empowering anointing begins to flow, you have to stay in the high place. Don't let it descend into lower levels. I'll give you an example from the Bible. In Luke 8, Jairus came to the Lord, and the anointing was flowing. The Master was right there with him, and his faith was high. Then the woman with the issue of blood came and touched the hem of the Lord's garment.

> And a woman having an issue of blood twelve years, which had spent all her living upon physicians, neither could be healed of any, came behind him, and touched the border of his garment: and immediately her issue of blood stanched. And Jesus said, Who touched me?
>
> —Luke 8:43–45

The woman's interruption caused Jairus to experience a break in his faith. The Lord noticed that Jairus was weakening.

Then they came and told Jairus, "Your daughter's dead. Don't bother the Master." By that time, the man's faith was on the floor. What did the Lord Jesus do? Two things. First, He said, "Don't give up; hold on to the little bit of faith you have." Then the Lord Jesus had seen how Jairus' faith weakened when the woman talked too long, and then it dropped lower when they came and said, "Your daughter has died. Don't bother the Lord." But the Lord protected Jairus' faith by saying, "Hold on. Don't give up." He went to the house and only allowed Peter, James, John, and the family to come in, to protect Jairus' faith.

Jesus went inside the house and said the little girl was only sleeping. The mourners all laughed at Him and mocked Him for saying that. Immediately He sent them all outside too. Why did He move them out? Because they were affecting the anointing, and because the faith of Jairus was almost gone, the Lord did what was necessary to protect Jairus' faith.

When I would minister in the crusades, if someone's testimony went on too long, it would affect the atmosphere. The flow would slow down. You may stop that person and pray for them, or you may simply stop them and go to someone else. You have got to keep the flow going, or before long, the flow will stop completely.

Sometimes the empowering anointing will move quickly; sometimes, it will move slowly. Sometimes it's a strong wind, sometimes it's a gentle wind, but it's still wind. It's still blowing. It's not gone yet. It's there. The wind hasn't stopped. It may stop if you allow it. It may stop if you resist the Spirit of God. It may stop if someone else tries to resist what's happening and you allow them to resist. You cannot do that. You have to control the flow so that you can continue to minister freely.

Now you will sometimes feel the anointing speed up, just like wind picking up and blowing harder. You've got to move quickly with it, just like Philip, who ran to meet the eunuch. He had to run to catch up and get into the chariot. The second he got in, what was the eunuch reading? Isaiah 53. What if Philip had walked instead of running? He might have missed the moment to change someone's life. Sometimes God says, "Let's go!" That's why you'll see me and others moving like a train in a service, not to lose the moment that could change the lives of thousands in that auditorium. And you can apply this same principle to whatever type of ministry you do for the Lord.

These chapters have taught you how to siphon the empowering anointing of God. That anointing on us is essential to ministry. After we siphon it by surrender, we maintain it with worship. Worship brings us into that manifestation of the Lord. Our surrender releases the power of the Lord, and now we maintain it in the atmosphere of worship.

We have to stay in the high places to keep the anointing of God flowing. If you want God to use you, it's your duty—just as it is my duty still to this day—to protect what God has given you. Read the next chapter, about protecting the empowering anointing, carefully. You won't find this information anywhere else.

Chapter 17

PROTECTING THE PURITY OF THE ANOINTING

I HAVE DEALT WITH this topic publicly but never in the way that I will deal with it in this chapter. I've seen God use many people in powerful ministry, and the only people who last, the only people who don't get taken off track or have their anointing diluted by mixing it with things of the flesh are people who learn to purify and protect the anointing.

Remember, spending time with the Lord Jesus is all that is required for the abiding anointing to operate. This inner anointing does not grow at all. Your hunger grows, your faith grows, and your love for the Lord grows. But the abiding anointing *in* you is always at full capacity.

The empowering anointing for ministry is different. It can intensify or diminish. It can grow or it may weaken. Not every Christian receives the empowering anointing. This outer anointing is only received after the Lord Jesus trusts us with it. As people He has entrusted with His power, we need to keep the empowering anointing pure from pollution.

Now let's talk about something that greatly affects the empowering anointing. If the believer becomes distracted and neglects his time with God—he is no longer paying the price, he is not giving Jesus the time He deserves, the time that belongs to Him—then the Lord will slowly distance Himself as the believer pulls away. The Lord never removes His presence quickly from any one of us. He will remove it very slowly. When He removes His presence from anyone, it is because that one is not giving God his time; as a result, his hunger level goes down, his faith decreases, and his love diminishes.

The Lord gives us time to get back into His presence so our hunger, faith, and love will keep growing. Continuing to neglect this time has a very high price. When a believer keeps neglecting to practice His presence, that precious presence will diminish. As we begin to pull away a little more, the result is less hunger, less faith, less love. This can result in even more pulling away from God, resulting in much less hunger, much less faith, and much less love. If we pull away completely, there is no hunger whatsoever anymore. Instead of growing, faith is dying. The heart becomes cold like ice.

Now, the danger deepens. The believer has become weak in his spiritual life. The Lord's presence within him has diminished because he has neglected the Lord, and now the empowering anointing will crush him because there is nothing in him that supports it. The empowering anointing remains because that is His gift, and a gift is not removed. Romans 11:29 tells us, "For the gifts and calling of God are without repentance." This means that the gift will remain in operation, even though the believer's life has become weak.

What happens when the burden of the empowering anointing becomes difficult to carry because the Lord's presence has diminished? The spiritual gifts and the empowering anointing that were given for ministry now become a heavy load, having no support from within, and now have the potential for destruction. The same gift that God gave to bless His people now becomes a burden too heavy to carry. The individual begins to hate their ministry, to despise the call. And now he wonders what he is going to do with himself. It becomes nothing more than a business proposition. There is now a temptation to start to sell the anointing or make merchandise of it. It's not for the Lord Jesus anymore. It has become *all about you*, since without His presence and His power, *you* is all that is left.

The Lord's presence is no longer in the believer's life at this point, so there is no longer any conviction. He allows things to pollute, dilute, or taint the empowering anointing and the spiritual gifts God has entrusted to him. Sin has now become rooted in his heart. The empowering anointing still flows, yet the Lord's presence is not there, so what he produces is empty and devoid of any real power. Every spiritual gift God has given him still operates, but the Lord is no longer using him; it is *the gift* that is using him.

That is why you must protect the empowering anointing in your life. *Make time with God your highest priority.* Never allow yourself to neglect the Lord, even though He is gracious and merciful. It is true that He does not remove His presence from you quickly, but why would you want Him to remove it at all? You know that He will give you time to wake up and repent, but why should that time be wasted? Better to continually put your best effort into maintaining this vital connection with the Lord so that you will always have a strong foundation for your ministry.

Remember, there is a price to pay for the empowering anointing, and it is spending time with the Lord, which is a privilege. It is a price that some are not willing to pay, and as a result, they allow the anointing on their life and ministry to become polluted. The pure anointing of God flows through them but then it becomes polluted by what they have allowed into their heart. It is now a mixture, impure and therefore weak and powerless. That is why the Lord has a process for keeping the empowering anointing pure.

THE LORD'S THREE-STAGE PROCESS FOR KEEPING THE ANOINTING PURE

Now, when you read that this is a three-stage process, you might get the impression that these are three quick steps to get you back on track. You would be mistaken. In our modern mindset we have become accustomed to getting quick fixes, easy answers, and simple solutions that cost us nothing and take little or no time or effort. God's kingdom does not operate that way. His precepts are serious business.

The three steps of His process for purifying the anointing are beating, shaking, and crushing. Do these stages make us want to give up? You bet they do. Just reading the words "beating, shaking and crushing" draws up images of painful corporal punishment. *That is not what this process is. God is not out to get us.* Watching my friends Oral Roberts and Rex Humbard navigate through the sometimes treacherous waters of a life in ministry gave me the wisdom and strength to not give up. I was very troubled by the process of God purifying His anointing in me, not realizing God was protecting my future. Now I can look back and thank the Lord for it because I know it is the reason that I am still here.

Beating, shaking, and crushing are the three stages an olive tree goes through before the olive oil flows. Before the olives fall, the tree is beaten with a rod. Then the tree has to be roughly shaken by hand for the olives to fall on the ground. After this, the olives are crushed. The olive oil never flows without these three steps happening. Let me share how each stage applies to God's process for purifying the anointing.

1. The beating stage

The Book of Deuteronomy talks about the beating of the olive tree.

> When thou beatest thine olive tree, thou shalt not go over
> the boughs again.
>
> —Deuteronomy 24:20

What is the beating process? In my opinion, it is coming to the cross where the flesh must be crucified. It is the work of the cross of Jesus in the lives of the ones God wants to use. If you want God to use you, the flesh must be put to death. Like the olive tree, you will be beaten by the work of the cross.

When we fully embrace the Lord's discipline, we must realize that we are also fully embracing His processes, including correction. Just as a child knows a parent who brings correction does it for their benefit, to train them and help them, we must trust our loving God and learn to love His correction. I have said to the Lord many times, "You can chastise me all You want; just don't ever leave me. You can correct me anytime, Lord. Just never leave my life." I can tell you He has answered this prayer quite well!

If we want to serve the Lord, we must be willing to take up the cross, deny ourselves, and surrender ourselves to Him. We are required to do this if we are to advance to a level of serving, not being served. This must be done before God can purify us. The apostle Paul understood this. In 1 Corinthians 9:27 he tells us:

> But I keep under my body, and bring it into subjection: lest
> that by any means, when I have preached to others, I myself
> should be a castaway.

Paul understood that he had to bring his physical body under subjection to the Holy Spirit, to maintain control over it lest he himself become disqualified from God's anointing. He knew that in order to do that, he had to crucify his flesh, deny the fleshly impulses it had, and force his lower nature to obey the Lord completely.

Why were olive trees beaten? So the olives that were ready to be crushed would fall. Only olives that were ripe enough would fall. The shaking mentioned by the prophet Isaiah came next.

2. The shaking stage

> Yet gleaning grapes shall be left in it, as the shaking of an olive tree.
>
> —ISAIAH 17:6

They shook olive trees. Why? So the ripe olives would fall, and they could use them. In our lives, the shaking is persecution. People will call you names. They might call your children names. They might even protest outside your house, as they did mine for years. If you have a public ministry, you might be attacked in the news, and you'll surely get some nasty comments on social media.

Shaking is a necessary step for our humility and repentance before God. We must come to Him in true repentance, our hearts broken by the very sin we have allowed. Denying ourselves and taking up our cross produces this humility and true repentance in our lives.

> For thus saith the high and lofty One that inhabiteth eternity, whose name is Holy; I dwell in the high and holy place, with him also that is of a contrite and humble spirit, to revive the spirit of the humble, and to revive the heart of the contrite ones.
>
> —ISAIAH 57:15

Shaking will come to each one of us, but what about the crushing?

3. The crushing stage

This is the one nobody likes because people don't realize the beauty of the scriptural principle that allows the crushing. Here's what Micah says:

> Thou shalt sow, but thou shalt not reap; thou shalt tread the olives, but thou shalt not anoint thee with oil.
>
> —Micah 6:15

In Israel, they tread or crush the olives in an olive press with a massive stone, not with their feet like grapes. In our lives, the crushing is total surrender to the Master and His will, no matter what His will is. You become willing to give up everything you love in life. You give up everything you want to hold on to because the Lord crushes it out of you. The crushing presses everything out of you that is worldly and would hinder God's plan for your life.

The crushing part of the purification process sanctifies you for the Lord's use. In this step He removes everything in your life that was produced by the flesh and the world.

I often ask the Lord to do one thing for me: "Lord, anything You hate that is in me, take it out and kill it!" If it originates in the flesh, if it comes from the world and its ways, I do not want it. It cannot help me; it can only separate me from Him, and that I will not allow. I love Him too much to allow that to happen.

These are the keys to your survival as a believer and as an anointed servant of the Lord. You won't have to worry about worldly pollution or the demonic, nor will you have to worry about a weakness that you can't control, if you allow God to put you through this process. In 2 Timothy 2:20–21 Paul notes that there are two kinds of vessels in a house: gold and silver for honor and wood and earth for dishonor. If you want to be a vessel of honor, you will have to go through the process. There is no other way. God will keep you through it all.

Chapter 18

SIX THINGS THAT CAN WEAKEN THE EMPOWERING ANOINTING

IN ADDITION TO allowing God's purification process in your life, you must remain vigilant about six key things that can weaken the empowering anointing on you. Now, you might be thinking, "But Pastor Benny, doesn't my anointing stay strong and pure as I spend time in the presence of God?" Absolutely, and I'll cover other things that keep it strong later in this chapter. The Bible says we are to resist the devil, but it says resist *not* the Holy Spirit, grieve not the Holy Spirit, quench not the Holy Spirit. Why? The Holy Spirit is as gentle as a dove, and He will not stay if there's a challenge. These are things about the anointing that few understand and even fewer teach or preach about, but *you need to grasp them if you want God to use you in ministry.*

1. ENTERTAINING THE DEMONIC

The empowering anointing loses its center, its power, its effectiveness when people entertain the demonic. How do they entertain the demonic? They allow demonic things into their lives, like Achan in Joshua 7, who took some kind of a demonic image and hid it in his tent in direct violation of what God had instructed. As a result, in verse 12, the Lord said, "Neither will I be with you any more, except ye destroy the accursed from among you." That is a revealing verse. The Lord withdrew His presence and His power from an entire nation because of one man's sin. One man caused a nation to lose a battle they could have won with only three thousand soldiers.

A cursed object brings a curse on someone's life and ministry. It can weaken the anointing, and if it is not dealt with, it can remove God's presence altogether. "Neither will I be with you," means God withdrew His presence. Why? Because the Holy Spirit is too holy to be around something that is demonic.

Sadly, many Christians cannot be used by God because they have demonic books and materials in their homes or watch things on TV that are demonic in nature. In addition, some pastors allow things in their ministry that are demonic in nature—either knowingly or unknowingly.

Deuteronomy 7:25 says, "The graven images of their gods shall ye burn with fire: thou shalt not desire the silver or gold that is on them, nor take it unto thee, *lest thou be snared therein*." Things you wear on your body can weaken the anointing. They can trap you in bondage. You do not realize how important this is to God. Christians may unknowingly wear demonic emblems—something on a watch or jewelry, insignias or logos on clothing—and they wonder why God doesn't use them. He's too holy to allow it, that's why.

Verse 26 says, "Neither shalt thou bring an abomination into thine house, lest thou be a cursed thing like it: but thou shalt utterly detest it, and thou shalt utterly abhor it; for it is a cursed thing." So get it out of there.

Spiritual warfare is real. We must stop allowing the enemy access into our lives. Whatever might be in your house that represents the demonic, get it out of there now. Don't waste any more time! They might be decorations or incense. It might be movies or TV shows you watch or music you listen to. Get rid of it. God has given you a priceless gift. Don't let anything weaken it. Get rid of all that stuff. You don't need it.

Now let me share another powerful truth: removing it is not enough. After you remove it, you have to speak to it. Most people do not do this, but it is in the Word. God's instruction in Isaiah 30:22 says, "Ye shall defile also the covering of thy graven images of silver, and the ornament of thy molten images of gold: thou shalt cast them away...*thou shalt say unto it, Get thee hence.*"

You have to speak and say, "Get out! I break the influence that was brought into this room. I command the demon that came with it to get out." You have to realize that object brought a demon with it. Now it is time to cast that thing out. It is not enough just to throw the object out. You have to throw the devil out with the object, and you do that with your mouth.

The Bible says that deliverance will come through your lips. Proverbs 12:6 says, "The words of the wicked are to lie in wait for blood: but the mouth of the upright shall deliver them." It comes when you speak it. You bring deliverance with your words. After that the empowering anointing can flow.

2. ALLOWING THE FLESH TO POLLUTE IT

The second thing that weakens the anointing is the flesh. God says in Exodus 30:32, "Upon man's flesh shall [the oil of the anointing] not be poured." He is saying, "Don't let the flesh interfere. Don't let your carnal nature and the world get in there."

The presence of God and the power of God in our ministries can weaken if we allow pollution in our lives. We cannot allow that pollution, no matter what it is. I had to learn to be careful who we talk to before we minister. Every hello could cost me because it could weaken the anointing. When someone opens their mouth—even a well-meaning Christian or pastor—it can bring the world into the conversation.

I also had to learn that you cannot allow yourself to get close to ungodly people. They will weaken the anointing on your life and bring you to a place where you may lose it altogether. Hollywood is a very tempting world, and I was foolish enough years ago to think I could minister to that world. I was invited to Hollywood parties to pray, and many of those in attendance were famous people. It was very attractive to me at that time. But I began to notice that things started to dissipate in my own life. Finally, my wife, Suzanne, asked me what I was doing. "Well, I want to win them," I told her. "They're interested in the supernatural. They want to know if what I do is real."

But Suzanne said, "You'll never win those people. That is not your call, Benny." She reminded me of the scripture that says, "Be ye not unequally yoked together with unbelievers: for what fellowship hath righteousness with unrighteousness? And what communion hath light with darkness?...Wherefore come out from among them, and be ye separate, saith the Lord, and touch not the unclean thing; and I will receive you" (2 Cor. 6:14, 17).

God will not permit uncleanness. If you allow it into your life, He will not use you. Just get it out. I learned this the hard way, but I am warning you in order to prevent you from going through some of the same things.

The empowering anointing can also be affected by the pictures you're looking at. I'm talking about anything ungodly. When I went to Madison Square Garden, photos of entertainers who had performed at the Garden were hanging all around. I said, "I don't want to look at their faces because it will weaken the anointing when I walk on the platform. Cover them." My staff put black curtains over each one of them.

Before I walk into hotel rooms, I have someone go ahead of me, and if there are any pictures on the wall that represent the world or the devil, they remove them. They take all the magazines and newspapers out of the room too. They go through the drawers and clean everything up. I don't want to see it. It weakens the anointing. I unplug the TV and radio. I don't want anything on when I walk in. I don't even want to hear soft worldly music when I come in. Why? To protect the anointing.

To some this might seem extreme, but not to me. I feel tremendous responsibility for the empowering anointing that will flow through me to touch others. I am in charge of its growth or weakening. I am in charge of increasing it or decreasing it. I am in charge of polluting it or keeping it pure. God puts me in charge, and I must protect it. Let me encourage you: you can do this. In Philippians 4:13 God promises you can do all things through Christ Who strengthens you!

3. Allowing the Anointing to Be Imitated, Borrowed, or Stolen

The anointing on you for your ministry or office is the only anointing you can release. You cannot release the anointing inside you, the abiding anointing. You can only release the one on you, the empowering anointing. Releasing it to the right people is the key because this anointing weakens when you release it to undeserving individuals.

> This shall be an holy anointing oil unto me throughout your generations. Upon man's flesh shall it not be poured, neither shall ye make any other like it, after the composition of it: it is holy, and it shall be holy unto you.
>
> —Exodus 30:31–32

When you allow someone to copy you, you've just weakened your ministry. I'm not talking about someone copying you without you knowing; you have no control over that. I'm warning you about letting others copy you by training them to be another you. There is no other you. There's only one you.

You can teach them, bless them, and instruct them. But the second you train or teach someone to copy you, you've just weakened your office. People always think, "If I have someone copying me, it will increase what God gives me." No, it doesn't. You are giving it away. Let me share how I learned this.

I used to have a class where I trained teams of people to work in my crusades and many churches where I would go. In these training sessions, I said, "Here's what I want you to do. You show up two hours before the crusade starts. While the crowd is getting in there, you choose a section of people. You start building faith in those people. You ask them what they are praying for and begin to sow the Word. Go to the next person and the next and the next. Sow the seed of the Word of God to at least fifty people and build their faith for two hours. Then when the worship starts and the anointing flows," I told the trainees, "run like fire and pray with the people you gave the Word of God to earlier."

The miracles started flowing during that season because the ministry teams sowed the seed of the Word, and the crowd was ready. It seemed like a great idea until some of those trainees began to think, "I have my own healing ministry now." It would have weakened the ministry, so I had to say, "No, you don't. You have been flowing under the anointing of this ministry. It's not yours."

If other people think it is theirs, they will make a mess. If you do not protect your anointing, people will steal it and weaken God's power on your life. Not only that, but it will also bring division and confusion to the body of Christ.

As I mentioned, you can release this anointing to others, and there are times when God will instruct you to lay hands on someone and release your anointing on them. If God has instructed it, as He instructed Moses to lay hands on Joshua, then He has a plan to raise up that other person without detracting from your calling. But don't do it just because you like the individual, no matter who they are. If God has not told you to do it, it will weaken your ministry.

4. ALLOWING THE WRONG PEOPLE TO GET CLOSE TO YOU

The people you allow to be close can fight God's plan for you and weaken the empowering anointing on your ministry. If you have people on staff in wrong positions or promote them to positions God hasn't called them to, it can cause division and hinder the anointing God put on your ministry or office. Maybe you're not leading a full-time ministry, so you have no staff or board members; it can still bring weakness to your ministry if there is strife and fighting among your family or other Christians who come alongside you in your work for God.

If you're going to be in ministry, you have to be aware of everyone around you and whether or not their spirit is flowing with your anointing. Sometimes you can tell outwardly right away if they are not with you; other times, you must ask the Holy Spirit to help you discern whether they are flowing in the same stream. If they are not, they will weaken the anointing on you.

If you have a teaching ministry, pay attention to who sits on the platform with you and sits on the front row listening to you. Why? Because the anointing can be affected by people challenging it. It is a challenge to go to churches with people sitting on the front row who will not worship. They just stare. That kills the anointing. When the Lord went to Nazareth in Matthew

13:54–58, they challenged Him. The Bible says Jesus could not do mighty works there. Why? He was challenged. He was opposed.

The abiding anointing is dependent upon *your* spiritual hunger. The empowering anointing is dependent on the need or the spiritual hunger of those you minister to. It is also affected by who is around you. When there is unity and harmony, it will increase on you. When there is division or disloyalty, it will diminish on you.

5. Controlling Spirits

In 3 John 1:9, John warned the church about a controlling man named Diotrephes, who wanted preeminence. He was trying to control people's lives with his religious spirit. If you let someone around you with a religious spirit, they will weaken or kill what God has given you. Legalistic, controlling men and women are deadly to the empowering anointing of God on you.

This happened to me. A friend of mine began to interfere, and I had to say, "Don't ever call me back again." I had to shut him out because I knew that allowing someone with a legalistic spirit, a religious spirit, is deadly to the anointing. Religious spirits will weaken and even kill the anointing. If you allow them near you, they will destroy the empowering anointing on you.

If you want God to use you in any type of ministry, *you must be careful not to replace the voice of the Holy Spirit with another person's voice.* Also, don't let a gifted person who believes he is a prophet become God's voice. That's very dangerous because you become more dependent on what God is telling him or her than what God is telling you. Eventually, you will have no ability to hear God for yourself. You must not allow the voice of God to be silenced in your own life by the voice of someone who believes he or she is a prophet. Eventually they will think they are speaking to you on God's behalf. The Lord does not need anyone to speak on His behalf. He can speak quite clearly to each one of us Himself.

6. Other People's Sin

If the wrong people touch you, they'll weaken the anointing on you. It says in 1 Timothy 5:22, "Lay hands suddenly on no man, neither be partaker of other men's sins: keep thyself pure." So don't lay hands on them—and don't even let them touch you lest you partake of their sin and impurities. Protect yourself from the danger, the witchcraft, and the demonic they bring with them.

A long time ago, just before God released the anointing on me greatly in Canada, I was in a store on a Monday night. A witch was shopping in the store, and she came up to me. Those devils know, and they told this woman who I was. She tried to touch me, and as I pulled away, I said, "Don't you touch me, lady." I felt something pulling out of me whenever that woman came near me. I got out of that store fast because I felt it. You can feel the demons in other people.

You even need to protect yourself from well-meaning people who want to pray for you and lay hands on you. I began learning these lessons when I would go to various meetings. Before the meeting, people would gather around and say, "Let's pray for Brother Benny." But when they laid their hands on me, I could feel the empowering anointing weakening. I have learned to not let anyone I do not know lay hands on me. The Bible says, "Know them which labour among you" (1 Thess. 5:12). Oral Roberts, Rex Humbard, and other men and women of God I know have prayed for me many times, and it was precious and blessed me.

It happened to me in Jerusalem in 1977. I got to the location where I would be ministering, and I let people pray for me. I felt the empowering anointing leaving me. Because I was already at the location and couldn't go back to my hotel, I had to get back on the bus, ask the bus driver to lock it, which he did, and intercede and pray until the anointing came back on me. I had to ask God to forgive me for being foolish enough to let people touch me, because some of their stories were crazy, and then they laid hands on me right before I ministered. I realized I should not let them touch me because I did not know what spirit was there. That is when I understood why I would sometimes see Kathryn Kuhlman pull away from people on the platform when she ministered.

As I was still learning, I would walk into those meetings and say, "Father, I apply the blood of the Lord Jesus on me right now," because I did not know what they did that day. I did not know what was in the atmosphere, but I knew I did not want the empowering anointing to be affected by it. Eventually, I learned to say, "Don't touch me, please. I don't need you to pray for me. I'm all prayed up." I did this to avoid the pollution that can get in there. God's Spirit is too holy to allow pollution around Him.

Conversely, the same thing can happen when you lay your hands on someone else. The Bible has a lot to say about laying hands on people. Frankly, it's forbidden to do so casually. Look again at 1 Timothy 5:22, which I quoted earlier. Paul told Timothy not to lay hands on anyone suddenly because you do not know what spirit is at work in them. Timothy was not living in sin. He wasn't weak in the Spirit, yet Paul warned him about this. Even though you're strong, please do not touch them. It will weaken your empowering anointing, and beyond that, think about the damage it can do to your life. I have seen ministers destroyed and ministries vanish because they did not heed Paul's warning.

Paul said not to lay hands *suddenly*. That means to use wisdom. Protect yourself before you lay hands on them. *Suddenly* does not mean you are not to lay hands on anyone ever, but do it with wisdom and be led by the Holy Spirit. Paul cautioned Timothy to use wisdom in laying hands on anyone. Sometimes under the empowering anointing, you can be led by the Holy Spirit to lay hands on someone. If you are certain that you are hearing from

God, and you have used wisdom to protect yourself in advance, you can feel free to follow the Spirit's leading confidently, having no concerns about polluting the flow of God through you.

I have laid hands on thousands of people, but I have learned to protect myself. *My protection came when I would spend time with Him.* The Lord's presence is my protection.

> Thou art my hiding place; thou shalt preserve me from trouble; thou shalt compass me about with songs of deliverance.
>
> —Psalm 32:7

Chapter 19

SEVEN THINGS THAT PROTECT THE EMPOWERING ANOINTING

S O WITH ALL these things that can affect the empowering anointing, how do you stay strong? Great question. I have just shared six things that can weaken the empowering anointing. Now let me share seven things that will protect this anointing.

1. THE WORD OF GOD

> When I washed my steps with butter, and the rock poured me out rivers of oil.
>
> —JOB 29:6

When we spend quiet times with the Lord in His Word and prayer, there comes a moment when the Word of God begins to abide in our spirit being. Eventually, *God's Word will intensify the empowering anointing on your life and ministry.* Meditating upon the Word will lead to revelation. As revelation begins to flow, the empowering anointing on your life and ministry will be strengthened.

2. WORSHIP

You stay strong by staying in the high place of the Holy Spirit. Worship is so vital to the high place God wants you to stay in. Remember, the high place of Deuteronomy 32:13, which is the secret place of Psalm 91, is your place of protection. Worship creates an atmosphere of protection.

> He made him ride on the high places of the earth, that he might eat the increase of the fields; and he made him to suck honey out of the rock, and oil out of the flinty rock.
>
> —DEUTERONOMY 32:12

As you learn about things that weaken the anointing, you must also understand that *the anointing can be restored.* If you have allowed things to weaken your anointing, it can be restored. Worshippers are the only ones who can get there. How do you think I was able to restore what I had to learn the hard way? I'm a worshipper. I love to worship the Lord. Worshipping the Lord has been in my heart from day one and continues to be in my heart to this day. I love to worship our wonderful Jesus because I adore Him.

Worship creates the atmosphere for your protection. It keeps you in those high realms of the spirit, where you are siphoning the honey of the Word, and siphoning the oil of the anointing. When you worship the Lord, His presence manifests. The Lord becomes tangible. When you worship, you surrender; you yield your body. Now you keep worshipping because it's easier to keep yielding. Your protection is restored every time you are united to the Lord.

3. PRAYING IN TONGUES

I touched on this in an earlier chapter, but I will say a bit more here. Sometimes praying in unknown tongues becomes necessary to stay in the high place where the honey and the oil flow. When something decreases the empowering anointing, you have got to increase it and restore its strength. In my case, that mostly happens through worship, but there have been times I have felt I need to pray in tongues to restore that realm so that I am able to siphon the anointing again.

I learned this back in 1977 in Jerusalem when I had to get back on the bus. I got into worship on the bus and reunited with the Lord so powerfully. Then I began praying in tongues, and it grew faster and stronger. And when that happened, I felt the demonic world get very confused. I felt the devils go into confusion. I sensed it. That is because the second you go into tongues, the enemy doesn't know what to do. You cripple him. As I prayed in tongues on that bus, I felt like the Lord put chains on the demons, and I walked out free. It was an amazing experience.

Worship is essential, but sometimes, praying in tongues is necessary because then you will win the spiritual battle. Through worship, you reconnect with God, and through tongues, you confuse the enemy's camp. These two things will restore the anointing.

4. HAVING A WORSHIPPER WITH YOU

Now even though you're protected in the high place through worship, and the enemy is confused because you prayed in tongues, you are still going into the battlefield every time you minister. The enemy does not know what to do at the moment, but he is not a fool. He sees you starting to minister, and he knows how to get back at you. Trust me; he has a lot of experience in attacking the people God uses. He will try to weaken you again, and that is the time you must find a worshipper to connect with you.

What do I mean by that? Have someone close to you who is a worshipper, who will keep you united to the Lord and protect you. They can pray and do battle for you as you minister. You see, when I was on that bus, I was fighting spiritual warfare, but I did not realize it was affecting my physical strength, too. My physical strength was affected even though the empowering anointing on me was strong again. When that happened to me in Jerusalem, John Arnott from The Toronto Blessing was there. John used to work with me. I said, "Johnny, stay with me," and I clung to him. My strength was low because of the battle I had just fought on that bus, and I needed his strength to keep going.

If God uses you long enough, you will need this advice one day. You'll be thanking God that you have read this book. And the more you battle, the more you need it. Depending on the level of spiritual warfare that you face, sometimes you need more than one person.

Once I was ministering in Mumbai with 2.5 million people in front of me, and I started feeling demonic attacks. I turned around, and Suzanne and two other ladies were there. I said, "Ladies, come behind me now! Pray!" The spiritual attack I felt was intense, but I felt strength return as soon as they started praying. That's when I realized there are times we need the support of more than one person praying.

You can apply this principle to any type of ministry for the Lord. You've got to stay in that realm of worship and protection. If you are not able to stay there on your own, get someone who can help you stay there. Get a worshipper to go with you and pray while you minister, and you can connect through their strength. You might find that you don't need this on a regular basis. Still, sooner or later, there will be a time that you do—primarily if you minister in another country where you're battling different spirits.

When you sense this is happening, get someone you know and trust and say, "Pray for me." Have him or her stand behind you and pray as you teach, preach, evangelize, or pray for people. You will feel the strength and the flow coming from that person.

5. STAYING STRONG TO FINISH STRONG

Staying in the realm of the high places of God will require much from one who yields to the empowering anointing. It can take a toll on you physically as well as spiritually. As you learn to remain in the realm of the high places of God, you will come to appreciate the support of others. This is especially true after you've been ministering for an extended amount of time. When you begin the ministry you are doing, everything is intense. But after a while, even though you began from a point of strength, after you have been ministering for a long time, you will find your strength weakening. Maybe you experienced something similar in the anointing, and you had to get back to a place of strength. Now you're really tired. It's not easy to stay in the high place alone; having a worshipper at your side will help you regain and retain your strength.

You may also benefit from having someone to keep watch for distractions. If you are in a church, the ushers can help with this. You don't need crying babies or people moving around during services. Ringing cell phones disrupt the whole congregation. Someone walking up to you at the wrong time can also distract you. These interruptions are manifestations of the flesh, which attempt to limit the flow of God's holy power. Having someone to help keep distractions at bay allows the anointing to stay strong.

It is important that you finish your time of ministry strong. Win the lost, all the way through your time of ministry, increasing in intensity as you move ahead. Let the end of your ministry time become the strongest part of it. To finish strong, you need to stay strong in the Spirit.

6. Not Allowing the Flesh to Manifest

This one is a major issue. When the empowering anointing is flowing, people can mistake things done in the flesh for a move of God. This is because as this anointing is flowing, it stirs everything in them, the Spirit as well as the flesh. We see an example of this in 1 Samuel 19:24 when Saul tore his clothes off and lay down naked, yet he prophesied.

> And he stripped off his clothes also, and prophesied before Samuel in like manner, and lay down naked all that day and all that night. Wherefore they say, Is Saul also among the prophets?
>
> —1 Samuel 19:24

Why did he prophesy? The anointing can sometimes activate a dormant gift, and a gift is given without repentance. King Saul had a gift. The prophetic was already in him. He prophesied when Samuel laid hands on him the first time, and that prophetic gift did not leave.

God's gift was still in Saul, but at this time it was simply dormant. Later, when he came in contact with the anointing on Samuel, this gift came back to life, but the flesh came with it. The anointing reactivated the gift, but the flesh also stirred. As the flesh rises up, it tries to mimic the empowering anointing, usurping its place. The flesh acts as though it was the actual anointing of God instead of a false, self-induced substitute.

Some people feel the wind of the Spirit blowing and start to manifest in the flesh. They start to say things that sound religious but are not of God. This interrupts what God is doing through you. Don't let this happen because it will weaken you. In Acts 16, when a demon-possessed girl started following Paul around and crying out every day that he was the servant of the Most High God, what did Paul do? He rebuked that demon spirit because he understood that was not the anointing. It was a manifestation of devils speaking through the flesh.

Paul saw the difference because what came out of this girl was just religious talk. Even though what she said about Paul was true, he discerned that it was a demon, a religious spirit that was speaking through her. Sometimes what someone says might be true, but the spirit behind it is a religious spirit. You cannot allow religious spirits to take over and dilute the power of God's anointing.

The flesh is not the Holy Spirit. People can start to do things that come across as religious. What they say may sound as though God is speaking, but it is not God. They will weaken the power of God flowing through you. Don't let that happen.

7. STAYING IN THE RIGHT STREAM

The empowering anointing can be affected negatively if you are around the wrong stream. Never accept an invitation from the wrong stream or the wrong river. What do I mean by that? The wrong stream or river is people and pastors who don't flow the same way you do.

You may try to minister in a church where the pastor disagrees with you being used by God with the Word of knowledge. He does not agree with different manifestations of the power of God. He does not support the way you flow in healing and the anointing of God. He has his own way, his own flow. If you want to minister in his church, you have to fit into his mold. He expects you to be like him.

If you accept that invitation, you waste your energy. Why?

Because the man who invited you is not in your flow. Here's one example from my life. I preached one time in a little country church in Canada. As the pastor opened the meeting, he said, "We're taking a chance today by having Benny Hinn." That was a signal that this was not a good idea. I got up, and it was tough. I could not minister freely because there was such a challenge in the atmosphere of that place.

After the service, as I went to my car, a sweet lady came up to me in the parking lot and said, "You feel like shaking the dust off, don't you?" Before I could answer, she said, "Well, I'm a Spirit-filled Charismatic. I was praying for you the whole time." And then she said something I have never forgotten: "I hope you've learned your lesson today." At the time, I didn't know what she meant, but now I do. Never go where they challenge you. If they don't flow with you, it can block the empowering anointing.

Finding the right stream is about finding people who believe the way you do about the anointing. I'm not talking about doctrinal differences among denominations. People may not see eye-to-eye with you on some points. Don't worry about differences in theology. It's the flow that matters. If you have the right flow, you will end up in the right theology. If you agree on the flow, you will find agreement on the theology later. But if you don't agree on the flow, you will never agree on the theology.

As you have been reading this book, I pray you have received wisdom about protecting the empowering anointing upon you for ministry. As you begin to be used by God more and more, He will reveal to you more of what He is about to do next in your life and in the world, for the day of the Lord is at hand. The prophetic gift will begin to explode inside of your spirit man.

At this level the prophetic gift falls under the covering of the empowering anointing. There is a stronger unction for the prophetic ministry that some are called to fill. This is the office of the prophet. Just because someone moves in a prophetic gift, it does not necessarily indicate that the person is called to the office of the prophet. This is a deep subject that requires careful examination of such a sensitive and important topic. To give this subject the focus and time it deserves, I have prepared a deeper teaching that I will share in the next part of the book. If you have a hunger to know more about the prophetic, this coming teaching will equip you for the call of God on your life.

PART III

ANOINTED TO PROPHESY

Chapter 20

THE MYSTERY OF THE PROPHETIC ANOINTING

T HE TIMES IN which we are now living are unlike any the world has ever known. There is an escalation in the intensity of spiritual battle in the heavenlies. Every nation on the planet is caught up in the prophetic unfolding of the end times before our very eyes. In these daunting days, in this prophetic climate, there has been an overabundance of people claiming to have a prophetic word to share, a warning or a decree that they say comes from God.

There is much today that is called prophetic that is not prophetic. So many voices in the world today claim to be prophetic voices, so many people claim to be prophets, but most of these do not even understand the office of the prophet, let alone have the anointing of God to hold such an office. Many are believers who have simply been misled about the anointing of the prophet, the gift of prophecy, and the office of the prophet, if they have been taught about such things at all. In this chapter we will begin building the foundation for a true understanding of the realms of the prophetic. You need a true understanding of the prophetic realms, and true understanding starts with the safe and secure foundation of the Scriptures.

The second chapter of Joel is often quoted in reference to the gift of prophecy, and rightly so. But there are three things this passage tells us about prophecy that most people miss. Let us take a deeper look at what this familiar Scripture is telling us.

First, Joel 2 declares that prophesying will take place "afterward." After what? To answer this, you have to look at what Joel said earlier. Joel 1:14 says, "Sanctify ye a fast, call a solemn assembly, gather the elders and all the inhabitants of the land into the house of the LORD, your God." God is asking His people to seek Him, call on Him, and cry out to Him. In Joel 1, God calls His people to intercession, and in Joel 2, He tells them what will come afterward. *Intercession gives birth to the prophetic.*

Second, in Joel 2:28 God says, "I will pour out my spirit." He didn't say pour *down*. If it was to be poured down, that would mean that He would be pouring it from heaven onto the earth. No, what Joel tells us here reveals that is not the case. *Pour out* means it's in your heart already. At salvation, the Lord already filled you with His Spirit. If you are saved, His Spirit is in you. Because the Holy Spirit is in each of us, *the prophetic is already in every believer.* It is already in you.

Third, God clearly states in verse 30, "I will shew wonders in the heavens and in the earth, blood, and fire, and pillars of smoke," which is judgment. To understand more about the prophetic releasing judgment, let's look at the Book of Acts. Peter quotes a passage in Joel 2 when he tells the crowd what happened on the day of Pentecost.

We're living in an exhilarating time for the church. There is no doubt that the Lord is restoring the gifts of the Holy Spirit. I believe the gifts are about to come into full operation, like we haven't yet seen, as it was two thousand years ago or in times past with different moves of God throughout church history. In order to prepare for these exciting days, we are in great need of a better understanding of the realms in which the prophetic anointing operates. Prepare now to plunge into the prophetic with me!

Chapter 21

FOUR REALMS OF THE PROPHETIC

S OME PEOPLE DO not believe the gifts of the Holy Spirit are for today, especially the prophetic, because of extremes they might have seen and because of Bible teachers that have dismissed the prophetic or any current proceeding word from God. The world's largest Protestant denomination states in its organization's doctrine that God no longer speaks to people past the last written Scripture. But the gifts of the Spirit are biblical, and their functions in the body of Christ have not ceased.

We know the prophetic is for our benefit because in 1 Corinthians 12:7 Paul says, "But the manifestation of the Spirit is given to every man to profit withal." Therefore, the prophetic is a must for our productivity in the Holy Spirit. The operation of spiritual gifts in your life is essential for the glory of the Lord to become manifest. If you want to fulfill all that God has called you to do, *you must embrace these gifts of the Holy Spirit*.

Let's start by looking at four different realms of the prophetic.

1. THE PROPHECY OF SCRIPTURE

The first prophetic realm is the Word of God itself.

> Knowing this first, that no prophecy of the scripture is of any private interpretation. For the prophecy came not in old time by the will of man: but holy men of God spake as they were moved by the Holy Ghost.
>
> —2 PETER 1:20–21

Peter calls it the "prophecy of the scripture" and clearly describes it as the declaration of the Word of God. It contains no error. It contains no mistakes. There are no imperfections in that realm of the prophetic. It is the inspired Word of God. It is divine truth given without human mixture. Nobody has added anything to Scripture and said, "Here's what I think it means." It is God's Word, pure and simple. God speaks it, and that's all there is to it. The Word of God is prophetic.

When people share scriptures, they are prophesying, whether they are aware of it or not. They're ministering in the first realm of the prophetic, because *Scripture is the first realm of the prophetic.* Every time in this book that I have quoted the Bible, I have prophesied to you. The entire Word of God is prophetic. The Word of God in Scripture is the first realm.

Only this kind of prophecy can rightly claim total inspiration by the Holy Spirit. All other realms of the prophetic are inspired, but they're not direct revelations from the Lord. With other realms of prophecy, the human element comes in to explain what God is saying. So when Peter said there's no private interpretation in the first realm, he implied that there could be private interpretation in other realms of prophecy.

The Word of God is the highest and the purest form of revelation and communication. Whenever God began to speak through a man, whether it was Isaiah, Jeremiah, Ezekiel, or another Old Testament prophet, they all said, "Thus says the Lord." None of them said, "I say" or "Let me explain it to you." These prophets in the Old Covenant days did not understand what they were saying. It wasn't their place to understand or explain.

Later on, when Lord Jesus came and gave us the Holy Spirit, the church began to understand what the prophets meant. We read in 1 Corinthians 2:9–10, "Eye hath not seen, nor ear heard, neither have entered into the heart of man, the things which God hath prepared for them that love him. But God hath revealed them unto us by his Spirit." God did not reveal them to the prophets of old—Isaiah, Jeremiah, and others. But He has chosen to reveal them to us.

When these Old Testament men and women of God prophesied, they did not know what they were saying.

> Of which salvation the prophets have inquired and searched diligently, who prophesied of the grace that should come unto you: Searching what, or what manner of time the Spirit of Christ which was in them did signify, when it testified beforehand the sufferings of Christ, and the glory that should follow. Unto whom it was revealed, that not unto themselves, but unto us they did minister the things, which are now reported unto you by them that have preached the gospel unto you with the Holy Ghost sent down from heaven; which things the angels desire to look into.
>
> —1 PETER 1:10–12

When you teach the Word of God, you know exactly what God is saying. Isn't that amazing? What a privilege.

2. THE SPIRIT OF PROPHECY

The second realm is the spirit of prophecy mentioned in Revelation 19:10:

I fell at his feet to worship him. And he said unto me, See thou do it not: I am thy fellowservant, and of thy brethren that have the testimony of Jesus: worship God: for the testimony of Jesus is the spirit of prophecy.

The "testimony of Jesus" is the preaching of the gospel under the anointing. When a person is ministering the gospel with power, the atmosphere becomes prophetic. That's what Scripture means by the spirit of prophecy. The Spirit of the Lord brings the atmosphere of the prophetic into a room.

The prophetic has an atmosphere. That atmosphere of the prophetic results from the Word of God being ministered with power, the gospel preached with power. Today, in many circles, people lack power. That's why in many areas there is no true prophetic gift in operation. And when there is no true prophetic gift, there are no other gifts in operation—no discernment, no word of knowledge, no word of wisdom. And there is no deliverance, no casting out demons either. Why is that? Because if there is no discernment, how can you discern the demonic to cast it out?

The prophetic is the greatest gift because it releases all other gifts. That's why Paul said, "Follow after charity, and desire spiritual gifts, but rather that ye may prophesy" (1 Cor. 14:1). When the prophetic begins to manifest, it activates all other realms. All other gifts come to life. When the prophetic begins, the word of knowledge is activated, the word of wisdom is activated, discerning of spirits is activated, the gift of tongues is activated. But it all begins with the prophetic. Therefore, the prophetic is the most important of all realms in our life. That's why Moses said, "Would God that all the LORD's people were prophets" (Num. 11:29).

Today, many do not want to allow the prophetic to flow because of confusion over what the prophetic is and how it should manifest and flow. Part of this is because we have not been properly taught how to control it. Once the prophetic flows, you have to control it, or it can get dangerous. People often want to get up and prophesy when I am under a heavy anointing in churches or crusades. But I have to say, "Not now," because I am still ministering the Word, and the Holy Spirit does not interrupt Himself. If I did not control that situation, I would have had all kinds of confusing things happen that could have been very damaging to the service and to the people attending. Paul's instruction to the believers in Corinth was, "For God is not the author of confusion, but of peace, as in all churches of the saints" (1 Cor. 14:33).

Why did this happen? Why did they feel led to prophesy? Because the prophetic is stirred when you preach the gospel under the power of God. The spirit of prophecy is mentioned in 1 Samuel 19 when Saul prophesied.

> And he [Saul] went thither to Naioth in Ramah: and the Spirit of God was upon him also, and he went on, and prophesied, until he came to Naioth in Ramah.
>
> —1 SAMUEL 19:23

The spirit of prophecy that came upon Saul continued for a long time. It permeated the atmosphere of the entire area just because of the spirit of prophecy flowing through the ministry of the prophet Samuel.

3. THE GIFT OF PROPHECY

Next, we have the gift of prophecy, which is the third realm. The gift of prophecy is mentioned in 1 Corinthians 12 and then explained more in chapter 14. It has borders, which means there are limits to its purpose. I'll explain in more depth about the borders on this gift at another time. For now I will share briefly with you the fourth realm, and then I will spend a large part of the next chapter on misunderstandings about this third realm, the gift of prophecy.

4. THE OFFICE OF THE PROPHET

Understand these two main points concerning the fourth realm of the prophetic: first, there is the office of the prophet, and next, the church is built upon this. Ephesians 2:19–20 says,

> Now therefore ye are no more strangers and foreigners, but fellowcitizens with the saints, and of the household of God; and are built upon the foundation of the apostles and prophets, Jesus Christ himself being the chief corner stone.

So here Paul tells us that apostles and prophets are the foundation that the church is built upon. We also read in Ephesians 4:11, "And he gave some, apostles; and some, prophets; and some, evangelists; and some, pastors and teachers." This verse clearly establishes that there is the office of the prophet.

Not everyone who prophesies is a prophet. Many can prophesy because they have received the gift of prophecy, but that is different from one who holds the office of the prophet. The prophet is the door to the prophetic. He or she is the one who brings that atmosphere into a room. That is what was going on in the lives of Elijah and Elisha in 1 and 2 Kings, where the prophetic was active in their followers. I'll be touching on the Scriptures that point to the office of the prophet later. The office of the prophet is a mighty office. God speaks through His prophets.

Chapter 22

MISUNDERSTANDINGS ABOUT THE GIFT OF PROPHECY

T HERE IS SO much confusion and danger today surrounding the third realm of the prophetic, the gift of prophecy. I will share what the Word of God says about the gift of prophecy for the rest of this chapter. Proper understanding always starts in Scripture. So let's start with Paul's explanation to the Corinthians.

> Now there are diversities of gifts, but the same Spirit. And there are differences of administrations, but the same Lord. And there are diversities of operations, but it is the same God which worketh all in all. But the manifestation of the Spirit is given to every man to profit withal. For to one is given by the Spirit the word of wisdom; to another the word of knowledge by the same Spirit; to another faith by the same Spirit; to another the gifts of healing by the same Spirit; to another the working of miracles; to another prophecy; to another discerning of spirits; to another divers kinds of tongues; to another the interpretation of tongues: but all these worketh that one and the selfsame Spirit, dividing to every man severally as he will.
>
> —1 CORINTHIANS 12:4–11

The Holy Spirit always provides the gifts to His church in perfection and order. When the Holy Spirit moves, there is no confusion. The gift of prophecy is given to exhort, to edify, and to comfort, which I will explain later in more detail. The gift of prophecy is living fire. The prophetic is the flame of Pentecost. It is what activates all other gifts.

Now, the gift must be judged. You and I are not permitted to judge the one who prophesies. We are, however, permitted to judge the gift. I'll repeat that because it is very important. *God does not permit us to judge the one God uses, but we are to judge the gift flowing in the church.*

Part of the confusion today is that people are judging those whom God uses. But we have no right to do that. We are to judge what they say; we are not to judge them personally. A big reason for the confusion is that people misunderstand what Paul says in 1 Corinthians 14:29, "Let the prophets speak two or three, and let the other judge." People read this and think, "Well then, I can judge prophets." No. Paul is talking here about the gift in operation. Note that the word *judge* in this passage does not mean to condemn; it comes from the Greek word *diakrino*, which means to discern, to determine, to separate thoroughly, to judge; in other words, to assess. We are to decide whether the words we are hearing line up with the Word of God. To understand Paul's meaning, you have to look at the whole chapter. Paul is talking about the gifts of the Holy Spirit and their operation within the church. He is not talking about judging the office of the prophet.

When Jesus instructed us in Matthew 7:1, "Judge not, that ye be not judged," the word *judge* here was translated from the Greek word *krino,* which means to judge judicially, to condemn, to decree, or to damn. We are never to condemn or damn anyone. Paul was not telling us to condemn the prophet; he was telling us to assess the prophetic Word.

If you look at the whole Word of God, both the Old Testament and the New Testament, you find that God will judge the prophet. "Rebuke not an elder" (1 Tim. 5:1) and "Against an elder receive not an accusation" (1 Tim. 5:19) are the instructions we read in the Scripture. You do not have the freedom to rebuke a man or woman of God. Biblically you have no right. God will judge you for it because you are attacking the office the Lord placed them in.

So when Paul says, "Let the other judge" (1 Cor. 14:29), he means you have the right to judge the words that are being spoken and say, "Does this line up with the Scripture?" Scripture is always our guaranteed guide.

THE OFFICE OF PROPHET

Now, let's focus on the holy side of the prophetic we operate in as the church. Please read Jeremiah 1:1–8. For the sake of space, I will only quote verses 9 and 10:

> Then the LORD put forth his hand, and touched my mouth. And the LORD said unto me, Behold, I have put my words in thy mouth. See, I have this day set thee over the nations and over the kingdoms, to root out, and to pull down, and to destroy, and to throw down, to build, and to plant.

Without the prophetic it won't happen. You have to speak it before God performs it. God told Jeremiah, "I'm putting My words in your mouth that you might be over the nations." That's a lot of power right there, and we can see the evidence today. Where is Babylon? Where is Assyria? Where is Edom, and where is Moab? Where are the Philistines? They're gone. Destroyed. Who destroyed them? God. How? When Jeremiah spoke it. God would not have done it had he not spoken it.

When he said, "To build and to plant," what was he talking

about? Israel. The Assyrians are gone. The ancient Greeks are gone. The pharaohs of Egypt are gone. Yet, there is massive proof that the Israelites are still here. That land is a reality called Israel. The Jews are a reality because God said, "I will not make an end of them."

Again, how did it all happen? Jeremiah spoke it, and God performed it. The prophetic is vital because when you speak it, God will do it.

But the prophetic is not always words. I encourage you to read the Book of Ezekiel and study all the things God had him do. The obedience of that man brought about the judgment of God. And it demonstrates that the prophetic is not always words. Sometimes the prophetic is expressed by an action, playing a part and doing things as a prophetic act. But this is true only when these things are done by the prophets.

This kind of prophetic releases the anointing of Isaiah 10:27, and the anointing of Isaiah 10:27 is the anointing that destroys and builds nations. Remember what I shared at the beginning of this book. There are three realms of the anointing: 1 John 2:27 is the abiding anointing that works in your heart. Acts 1:8 shows the empowering anointing for your ministry or office. And Isaiah 10:27 reveals the dominion anointing that destroys and builds nations. The dominion anointing transforms nations.

That dominion anointing is the anointing that came against the Assyrians. When Isaiah 10:27 talks about the yoke being broken, it refers to the yoke of the Assyrians, not a yoke on somebody's neck. So if you've ever quoted Isaiah 10:27 to declare God is breaking the yoke off someone's neck, I encourage you to reread Isaiah 10. God spoke of the Assyrians who came against Israel, and the anointing broke that particular yoke.

That dominion anointing is the anointing that worked in the life of Moses when he came into Egypt, destroying the land. That same anointing worked in the life of Joshua when he came into the Promised Land. So powerful was the anointing on him that he commanded the sun to stand still. What anointing is that? It's the anointing affecting the destiny of nations.

It is the same with Jeremiah's prophesying or acting. The dominion anointing starts to work through Jeremiah, eventually destroying the Assyrians and Babylonians.

The Roman Empire came crumbling down for one reason: Paul the apostle went to Rome, and his preaching destroyed the whole empire. That's what happened. He had to go to Rome in order to bring down a whole empire and to raise up the church. I will write more about the dominion anointing in later chapters.

God is revealing to us mysteries of the anointing and mysteries of the prophetic. "He that hath an ear, let him hear what the Spirit saith unto the churches" (Rev. 2:29).

Chapter 23

THE PROPHET AND GOD'S REDEMPTIVE PLAN

W E NEED THE prophets. Some prophesy. Some are prophets. There is a distinct difference between a person who operates in the gift of prophecy and one who functions in the office of the prophet. The prophet is the second office mentioned in the five ascension gifts that Jesus gave the church to mature us for the work of the ministry. The prophet is of paramount importance.

> And he gave some, apostles; and some, prophets; and some, evangelists; and some, pastors and teachers; for the perfecting of the saints, for the work of the ministry, for the edifying of the body of Christ.
>
> —EPHESIANS 4:11–12

When a prophet in the Bible, such as Isaiah, Jeremiah, or Ezekiel, prophesied, he stayed within God's plan of redemption. No matter what the subject, whether he spoke about the Israelites' sin or redemption, the prophetic word he spoke dealt with God's plan of redemption. After the prophets decreed that judgment would come upon the Israelites as a result of their sin, even when the prophets spoke of Babylon or other nations that God used to judge His people Israel, every word the prophets spoke was still within God's redemptive plan for Israel.

There are Scriptures that declare God raised up nations such as the Assyrians, the Babylonians, the Medes, and the Persians. They were raised to fulfill God's purpose: to fulfill God's redemptive plan for Israel. For example, God used the Assyrians as His rod of judgment to punish Israel for their idolatry. He also used the Assyrians to preserve Israel and ultimately to restore them.

God did the same thing with the Babylonians. He raised up King Nebuchadnezzar to judge Judah and to purify them. He later used the Medes and Persians to restore the people of Israel to their own land. All this was part of God's redemptive plan.

God also raised up Cyrus for His purpose in His redemptive plan. In Isaiah 45 it was Cyrus that was mentioned in this prophetic Word, hundreds of years before he was on the throne. God prophesied through Isaiah that Cyrus would be the one who would restore Israel to their homeland and to help them rebuild the temple. The common thread we see here is God's redemptive plan for His people. *The prophetic always stays within the border of God's redemptive plan.*

All four realms of the prophetic cannot go outside redemption. Every way you look at it, the Bible is the story of redemption. Look at the story of Abraham going into Egypt in Genesis 12:10–20. God caused Abraham to leave his home and go into the Promised Land, and then He caused Abraham to go into Egypt. You've heard the story before, how Abraham told Pharaoh about Sarah being his sister because he was afraid Pharaoh might want to kill him to take Sarah. Abraham actually spoke the truth. Sarah was his half sister and his wife; they shared the same father. God used Pharaoh to bless Abraham with gold and silver, to establish him in the Holy Land. This points to God's redemption plan.

We find another example of God's redemptive plan in Isaac's

life. In Genesis 26:1–16 we see the story of Isaac and Abimelech, king of the Philistines. Abimelech made a covenant with Isaac to protect him. Once again, God used an ungodly king so that His redemptive plan might be established through him.

In the life of Joseph, we find a third example of God's redemptive plan at work. Genesis 37–50 gives the complete story. The bottom line is this: God used Pharaoh to bless Joseph and save His people again. Every individual Gentile king that we see in these examples was raised up by God so that he could in one way or another fulfill God's redemptive plan for Israel.

God allowed the Philistines and their mighty champion Goliath to exist so that there could be a David—the same David we all know and love. The Philistines were used by God to promote David from shepherd to warrior to king; He used the enemy army and their champion to fulfill His redemptive plan. Read through the Bible with redemption in mind, and you will see that over and over again, God used men who were ungodly to stand in a position where they would fulfill God's redemptive plan.

In every example, we see that the prophetic word stayed within the borders of the redemptive plan. *When the prophetic goes outside of redemption, it goes outside of the Word of God.*

Chapter 24

UNDERSTANDING THE DOMINION ANOINTING

I SEE THE WORLD as a giant puzzle. Lately I have seen the pieces coming together, and it isn't very comforting. Understanding the dominion anointing spoken of in Isaiah 10:27 will help us understand the times and seasons we are now enduring, as well as the strategic place each of us holds as the coming days unfold.

As I said in chapter 2, very few people have the Isaiah 10:27 anointing. That anointing rested on Moses, Joshua, Isaiah, Jeremiah, Ezekiel, Elijah, Elisha, and a few others in the Old Covenant. It rested on individuals God used as mouthpieces through prophecy to raise a kingdom up or to destroy it.

To better understand what this rare and precious anointing is, let us take a closer look at the scripture that announces it.

> And it shall come to pass in that day, that his burden shall be taken away from off thy shoulder, and his yoke from off thy neck, and the yoke shall be destroyed because of the anointing.
>
> —ISAIAH 10:27

There are some misconceptions about this verse and what yoke is indicated here. But let us put our focus on the last word:

anointing. The word translated as "anointing" here is the Hebrew word *shemen;* it describes a particular type of olive oil, the kind that is scented with perfume. This implies a level of richness and rarity. This Hebrew word translated as "anointing" is used in Scripture only here; in other places in the Old Testament, the word *mischah* is most commonly used to refer to the unction for an office. This particular word infers that this special anointing is as rare as the costly perfumed oil that paints this picture.

The dominion anointing holds the potential for transformation on a global scale. In it is the power to break down nations and to build nations up, to uproot one form of government and transplant another in its place. Events on this scale are not commonplace, and the power to initiate such epic changes is tremendous, even awesome. It is not a power to be handled lightly; therefore, it is not given lightly. Just as the empowering anointing for ministry is not given to everyone but only to those who have proven themselves faithful and trustworthy through time spent in the presence of the Lord, so it is with this gift.

The abiding anointing is bestowed on all believers at the time of salvation. The empowering anointing is given to those whom God can trust with it. It is bestowed on those who have paid the price for this anointing to minister. The dominion anointing, however, comes only to a select few. Only a handful of prophets have reached this level. And there is good reason for that: with great power comes great responsibility. Only those who have shown themselves responsible at that level, such as Moses, Isaiah, or Ezekiel, will carry this heavy mantle of anointing.

I believe we are coming into what I call the Elijah realm of the anointing. The Elijah realm is a realm we haven't seen fully on earth yet. We have seen glimpses of it and seasons of it that came and went. It came, and it did not stay long. We are coming into the Elijah days very soon, a time when this tremendous power of

God will be displayed more than ever. During this season nations will be shaken on such a scale that it can only be seen as a global repositioning of governments. Only a pure anointing on your life can keep you during such a time.

Scripture helps you put the puzzle together because it connects what's happening in the world with what the Lord has foretold in His Word. I like to look first at what's happening in Israel, not just because it's the land of my birth but because it is the voice of prophecy. The voice of prophecy is not America, Russia, or China; it is Israel. Not only do you have to look at Israel, but you also have to look at what is happening in Europe and especially in the United Kingdom. America is not major when it comes to biblical prophecy; the part that this country plays is relatively minor. It has a part to play, but it is not a big part. When it comes to God's plan for the world, right now America is being moved out of the way prophetically. America will have its place still for a very short season, and I will write about America in biblical prophecy in a coming book.

You have to look at it all like a giant puzzle, and the center of it is the Bible. When you start looking at everything through the lens of God's Word, then you begin making the right connections and you can accurately put the pieces of the puzzle together. Start with searching the Scriptures to learn first about Israel, about its place in the world and its events, through the first realm of the prophetic, God's written Word. After you have that understanding, then you may learn about other nations and how they fit into the prophetic, according to Scripture. The picture is not complete yet. More and more will be revealed as things progress and develop because prophecy is revealed while it is in process. It is crucial that you understand your place in God's unfolding plan.

> But of the times and the seasons, brethren, ye have no need that I write unto you. For yourselves know perfectly that the

> day of the Lord so cometh as a thief in the night. For when
> they shall say, Peace and safety; then sudden destruction
> cometh upon them, as travail upon a woman with child;
> and they shall not escape. But ye, brethren, are not in dark-
> ness, that that day should overtake you as a thief. Ye are all
> the children of light, and the children of the day: we are not
> of the night, nor of darkness. Therefore let us not sleep, as
> do others; but let us watch and be sober. For they that sleep
> sleep in the night; and they that be drunken are drunken in
> the night. But let us, who are of the day, be sober, putting
> on the breastplate of faith and love; and for an helmet, the
> hope of salvation. For God hath not appointed us to wrath,
> but to obtain salvation by our Lord Jesus Christ.
>
> —1 THESSALONIANS 5:1–9

Now this tells us that God has given us light to know the seasons. If you are walking in His light, it will illuminate your understanding so that you clearly see and comprehend what Scripture
is revealing prophetically.

Another Scripture passage I would like you to read is found
in 2 Thessalonians. After you read this, we will show how this
Scripture fits together with 1 Thessalonians 5.

> Now we beseech you, brethren, by the coming of our Lord
> Jesus Christ, and by our gathering together unto him, that
> ye be not soon shaken in mind, or be troubled, neither by
> spirit, nor by word, nor by letter as from us, as that the
> day of Christ is at hand. Let no man deceive you by any
> means: for that day shall not come, except there come a
> falling away first, and that man of sin be revealed, the son
> of perdition; who opposeth and exalteth himself above all
> that is called God, or that is worshipped; so that he as God
> sitteth in the temple of God, shewing himself that he is God.
> Remember ye not, that, when I was yet with you, I told you

these things? And now ye know what withholdeth that he might be revealed in his time. For the mystery of iniquity doth already work: only he who now letteth will let, until he be taken out of the way. And then shall that Wicked be revealed, whom the Lord shall consume with the spirit of his mouth, and shall destroy with the brightness of his coming: even him, whose coming is after the working of Satan with all power and signs and lying wonders, and with all deceivableness of unrighteousness in them that perish; because they received not the love of the truth, that they might be saved. And for this cause God shall send them strong delusion, that they should believe a lie: that they all might be damned who believed not the truth, but had pleasure in unrighteousness.

—2 THESSALONIANS 2:1–12

Paul states that two things must happen before the Lord returns: (1) a falling away, and (2) a revealing of the man of sin. Paul told the people in Thessalonica nearly two thousand years ago to be prepared. They were expecting to see something, but they all died and did not see it come to pass. But I believe this generation will.

Chapter 25

THE DOMINION ANOINTING REVEALED

THROUGHOUT GOD'S PRECIOUS Word we have examples of the dominion anointing that conquers kingdoms and establishes nations. These biblical world changers will be followed by amazing leaders of later church history, all the way into the twentieth century. The dominion anointing is shown by example throughout this exciting chapter. All of them have been selected because of the impact they made in their world because of the dominion anointing.

BIBLICAL EXAMPLES OF THE DOMINION ANOINTING

Of course, the Lord Jesus operated in this anointing, but in Him all the anointings of God abide and find their fullness because He is Christ, the Anointed One. He was present in the lives of each of these anointed vessels. We will begin with one of the earliest examples of the dominion anointing.

Moses

The dominion anointing Moses carried delivered the children of Israel and crushed the armies of Egypt. The premier prophet of the Old Testament stood at the helm of God's power as He executed the ten plagues, which culminated in the destruction of the firstborn of Egypt and led to the release of the Hebrews from slavery. The nation of Israel was born, while the nation of Egypt was decimated. One was torn down and the other built up through the revelation of the dominion anointing.

Joshua

Joshua, the prophetic successor of Moses, was fiercely devoted, and his strength and courage elevated him to a position of God-ordained leadership. Joshua led the foundling nation of Israel in the conquest of the Promised Land. In Joshua 1:5 God tells Joshua, "There shall not any man be able to stand before thee all the days of thy life: as I was with Moses, so I will be with thee: I will not fail thee, nor forsake thee." Joshua commanded an army of former slaves and their offspring in an extended campaign of removing kingdoms and governments in order to establish territories for each of the twelve tribes. He was able to do this through the power of the dominion anointing working through him.

Deborah

Deborah was a force to be reckoned with. She was *fierce*. When Joshua completed his tenure, Deborah, a prophetess of God, led God's people as one of the first judges of Israel. (See Judges 4–5.) She gave a prophetic word to Barak the son of Abinoam to go up against the army of Jabin. This mighty man refused to go unless Deborah went with him. Barak indeed overcame the army of Jabin, but Jabin's captain Sisera was killed by a woman, Jael, who was honored in Deborah's song of victory. (See Judges 5.) Once again, the dominion anointing was in full effect, tearing down the kingdom of Jabin in favor of Israel.

Gideon

The reluctant warrior, the precautious prophet, and in his own assessment the least significant member of the smallest tribe of Judah, Gideon was still chosen by God. Gideon proved God's calling on him and accepted the dominion anointing he was designed for and destined to walk in. Judges 7 tells the story of Gideon's victory over the massive Midianite army with a whittled down band of only three hundred men from the initial strength of thirty-two thousand volunteer soldiers he commanded. The power of God flowed through Gideon to tear down, to build, and to take dominion.

Samson

Samson was Israel's own man of valor. Samson demonstrated supernatural physical strength and walked in covenant with God. Samson, a Nazirite, was dedicated to God from the womb. His barren mother received a visitation from the Angel of the Lord, who told her she would give birth to a son. He instructed that the boy's head was never to be touched by a razor, and he foretold that Samson would take the lead in delivering Israel from the hands of the Philistines (Judg. 13:1–5). Samson led Israel for twenty years in the days of the Philistines. The dominion anointing was strong in Samson's life. Once, the Spirit of the Lord came upon Samson, and he killed two thousand Philistines with the jawbone of a donkey. Even after Samson fell into lustful sin with Delilah and she cut off his hair, God was not through using Samson in a mighty way. Samson's power was disabled, and he was taken captive. Blinded and in chains, Samson pulled down the pillars of the temple of Dagon and killed thousands of Philistines who had gathered there. God restored Samson's strength, and he slew more Philistines at that moment than he slew in his entire life. (See Judges 16.)

David

David, the popular Sunday school hero, was so much more than the boy champion who defeated Goliath, the Philistine giant. David had a personal, loving, desperately dependent relationship with his Creator, his defense and his friend. God communed with David. David knew His Lord and King.

David was anointed king of Israel by the prophet Samuel when he was a young shepherd. Not even David's father, Jesse, saw the potential in his own son. He did not know David was even a possible candidate to be king. And neither did Samuel until God opened the prophet's eyes. David is our example that when people see a shepherd boy, God sees a king. David was a prophet and walked in the mighty dominion anointing as he battled the enemies of Israel. David and his kingdom enjoyed a rest from Israel's enemies at the end of this mighty king's reign.

Elijah

Elijah called down fire from heaven. The mighty Tishbite prophet first enters the Scripture in 1 Kings 17:1, where he proclaimed a prophetic word against Ahab and the nation of Israel: no rain except by my word. The drought of three years culminated in the famous showdown at Mt. Carmel, when Elijah destroyed the prophets of Baal. The great authority of the dominion anointing marked Elijah's life and ministry through the first chapter of 2 Kings, and in 2 Kings 2:11 his mantle was passed to his successor, Elisha.

Elisha

Elisha would not leave Elijah's side, knowing there was a mantle from his mentor that was waiting for him. Suddenly a chariot of fire and horses of fire appeared and separated the two of them, and Elijah went up to heaven in a whirlwind. The cloak fell from Elijah when he was caught up, and the dominion anointing of the prophet Elijah now rested upon Elisha as he picked up Elijah's cloak. Elijah's mantle now rested upon Elisha. Elisha walked in the dominion anointing all the remaining days of his life. When a dead man's corpse was thrown on Elisha's bones, the dead man was resurrected and stood to his feet because there was still sufficient power in the dead prophet's bones.

Peter

The apostle Peter, the disciple of Jesus Christ, began to operate in the powerful dominion anointing on the day of Pentecost, when the Holy Spirit was poured out. Peter's sermon beginning in Acts 2:14 culminates with the salvation of three thousand souls, as we read in verse 41. Peter walked in such authority that they laid the sick on mats on the city's pathways, hoping Peter's shadow would touch them. Jesus prophesied that His church would be built upon Peter's divine revelation of Jesus Christ. Peter was a significant leader of the believers of the early church and turned the world upside down with the gospel of Jesus Christ.

Paul

Born in Tarsus, Saul was an Israelite from the tribe of Benjamin and a Roman citizen. He was trained as a Pharisee, and he persecuted Christians. Saul was present at the stoning of Stephen. Saul was temporarily struck blind and was dramatically converted when he had an encounter with the resurrected Jesus on the road to Damascus. Throughout the Book of Acts the dominion anointing catapulted the newly named Paul to a seriously significant place in world history. The apostle Paul's missionary journeys changed the course of nations. Paul's Holy Spirit–breathed letters to early believers and church leaders comprise a major portion of the New Testament and still guide the lives of Christians all around the world today.

WORLD-CHANGING EXAMPLES
IN THE LATER CHURCH

In every generation since the first-century Christians, there have been people who were appointed by God to carry the rare and precious dominion anointing. I have chosen a few examples that are particularly noteworthy; it is by no means a comprehensive list. Some names may be familiar to you, while others may not. But whether or not you know these names, the impact they made is undeniable.

Jan Hus

The dominion anointing flowed through fourteenth-century reformer Jan Hus, changing the face of Western Europe and leaving a pathway for others in the Reformation period. His presence in the earth changed the direction of the church worldwide.

Hus was critical of ungodly practices in the Catholic Church, such as the selling of penance, positions, and sacred items for money. For his outspoken stance Hus was excommunicated and lived in exile for two years. While in exile he compiled his views on the church in a book titled *De Ecclesia*. He was then called before the Council of Constance in Germany, arrested, and jailed but refused to change his stand, saying, "I would not for a chapel of gold retreat from the truth!"

Hus was executed for heresy in 1415. Before his death he prophesied, "You are now going to burn a goose, but in a century you will have a swan which you can neither roast nor boil."[1] This prophecy inspired Martin Luther to adopt the swan as his symbol, which is still used by many Lutheran churches.

Martin Luther

About a hundred years later, the swan appeared when Martin Luther nailed his Ninety-Five Theses on the door of the Castle Church in Wittenberg, Germany.

Martin Luther was an important figure in the Protestant Reformation as he operated under the dominion anointing. While studying at a Catholic monastery, Luther became convicted by a principle he found in Scripture, "The just shall live by faith" (Hab. 2:4; Rom. 1:17; Gal. 3:11; Heb. 10:38).

Like Hus, Luther criticized the Catholic Church for its ungodly practices, and he historically nailed a list of his disagreements (the Ninety-Five Theses) to the door of the Wittenberg church in 1517. Copies in Latin spread throughout Europe, igniting the Protestant movement as the mighty dominion anointing continued to flow. Excommunicated from the Catholic Church, Luther organized a fledgling Scripture-based church, teaching and writing many hymns, including "A Mighty Fortress" and "Away in a Manger."

Moved by the Holy Spirit, Luther believed everyone should have access to Scriptures, so he translated the Bible into the common German language, printed in 1536. He died in 1546 and was buried at All Saints' Church in Wittenberg, where he had posted his Ninety-Five Theses almost thirty years before.

William Tyndale

"Let there be light." These powerful words near the beginning of the Holy Bible were penned by William Tyndale, whose translation of the Bible also brought us such terms as Passover, atonement, and "judge not that ye be not judged." Born in England around 1494, Oxford educated and gifted in theology and languages, Tyndale was a contemporary of Martin Luther, and like him Tyndale also operated in the dominion anointing and gave access to the Scriptures to the common man, changing the face of Europe and the world.

At that time it was illegal to even possess a copy of any Scripture that was not sanctioned by the Catholic Church. Fluent in Hebrew, Greek, and Latin, Tyndale began his own translation of the Bible around 1525 and completed it while hiding in Europe over the next ten years. Betrayed by a friend, in 1535 Tyndale was arrested for heresy and extradited to England, where he was convicted and executed in 1536.

The dominion anointing continues to flow through Tyndale's work; many Bible translations would not exist without Tyndale's translation of the Scriptures. Scholars estimate more than three-quarters of the King James Bible, first published in 1611, can be directly attributed to Tyndale's work.

John Wesley

The modern world was transformed by the dominion anointing that was fully functioning in John Wesley. He called himself "a brand plucked out of the fire" (Zech. 3:2). In 1709 he was stranded in his burning home until a man standing on the shoulders of another man lifted the five-year-old Wesley out of a window. This theologian and evangelist, along with his younger brother Charles, led a revival movement in the Church of England that became known as Methodism.

After a deep religious experience left his "heart strangely warmed,"[2] Wesley traveled the country on horseback to preach salvation by faith through God's grace as "free in all, and free for all."[3] In 1739 he and his brother organized the Methodist Society in England. Instead of large cathedrals, believers met in small chapels and were encouraged to actively care for the poor.

Wesley preached that all people were capable of receiving salvation and was also a strong opponent of slavery. His abolitionist teachings influenced many on both sides of the Atlantic as he flowed in the dominion anointing. He died in 1791 at age eighty-seven; his last words were, "The best of all is, God is with us."[4]

D. L. Moody

In his own words Dwight Lyman Moody said there were "few more unlikely" to become a Christian, let alone become an evangelist, teacher, and anointed man of God. Born in 1837 in Massachusetts to a difficult life of poverty, Moody became a Christian in 1855 when his Sunday school teacher talked to him about how much God loved him, moving him first to salvation and then into ministry. Moving in the dominion anointing, Moody displayed a tireless devotion to his congregants, which led to amazing church growth. President Abraham Lincoln once spoke at his Sunday school. During the Civil War, Moody visited the battlefront often, providing comfort and encouragement to weary troops. In 1864 Moody started the Illinois Street Church in Chicago; the Great Chicago Fire of 1871 destroyed the church and Moody's home, leaving him nothing but his Bible and his reputation. The next few years were a whirlwind of preaching expeditions as the dominion anointing led him across America, to the United Kingdom, and even to Sweden, where thousands often attended a single meeting. President Grant and members of his cabinet attended one of Moody's services and met with him privately.

Moody returned to Massachusetts and led a series of conferences for ministers and encouraged believers to serve in missions. Moody preached his last sermon in Kansas City, Missouri, in 1899 and died just a month later. The Moody Bible Institute (MBI), begun in 1886, is a fully accredited university, serving thousands of students every year on its three campuses in Illinois, Michigan, and Washington. It also includes Moody Radio, a network of seventy-one evangelical stations, as well as digital platforms, that continue to spread the gospel. Moody Publishers, another arm of MBI, remains a vibrant publishing house, representing a number of renowned authors and offering materials to support ministries around the world.

Albert Benjamin "A. B." Simpson

Fire begets fire. A. B. Simpson was on fire! He transformed the way ministries reach the lost. His approach focused on the common man and pointed to worldwide missions. The dominion anointing on his life changed the world.

Raised in a strict home with Puritan ideals, in 1859 the young Canadian teen began a fresh walk of faith, influenced by Irish evangelist Henry Guinness, who trained and sent hundreds of "faith missionaries" around the world. Later, while pastoring in Louisville, Kentucky, Simpson felt led to build a simple tabernacle to reach "the common man."

When Simpson moved to the bustling city of New York, the tremendous number of immigrants and the conditions in which they were living moved his compassionate soul-winning heart. Under the direction of the dominion anointing, he began the Christian and Missionary Alliance (CAMA), a training program to equip ministers for serving in missions to other countries and cultures. His teaching emphasized four aspects of Christ: "Jesus our Savior, Sanctifier, Healer, and Coming King."[5]

Simpson also composed more than one hundred hymns, such as "A Missionary Cry," which encourages bringing "the gospel of the kingdom" to every land.[6] He died in 1919 in New York, but the global outreach he launched influenced many later ministries and continues as his ongoing legacy.

William Franklin "Billy" Graham

Just as I am, without one plea,
But that thy blood was shed for me.[7]

This hymn was a favorite of American evangelist Billy Graham. It was often used as the invitation at the more than four hundred crusades he held in churches, tents, arenas, and stadiums around the world, reporting more than 3.2 million responses to altar calls across more than fifty years of ministry.

Sometimes known as "America's pastor," Graham traveled the world as the powerful dominion anointing opened doors to governments and leaders. He met with thirteen consecutive US presidents, from Truman to Trump. He also met with Queen Elizabeth II, Nelson Mandela, and a wide array of leaders from all corners of the globe.

Graham was a strong supporter of civil rights. During the 1950s he instituted a policy of racial integration for all of his crusade audiences. He invited Rev. Martin Luther King to join him on the platform and speak on several occasions. Graham also refused to hold crusades in South Africa under apartheid until integrated audiences were allowed.

Graham used radio and television to access larger audiences to hear his messages. By incorporating media outlets into his ministry, he was able to reach a worldwide audience. Graham famously instituted a code of ethics for his life and work in order to protect against accusations of financial, sexual, and power abuse. Vice President Mike Pence was known to be a follower of "the Billy Graham rule,"[8] using its principles to protect his own reputation.

Rev. Graham wrote thirty-three books, many of which were best sellers, including his autobiography, *Just as I Am*. He died of natural causes at his North Carolina home in 2018; he was ninety-nine. To this day the Billy Graham Evangelistic Association continues to be one of the largest evangelistic ministries in the world. Billy's son Franklin Graham heads Samaritan's Purse, which provides disaster assistance and humanitarian aid around the world.

Some two hundred thousand people visit the Billy Graham Library each year. Today his messages continue to reach people online, through radio, and in print. From the balcony of heaven, Billy Graham is still winning the lost.

Oral Roberts

"Go into every man's world." This is the direction that God gave to Oral Roberts, launching him into a worldwide, world-changing ministry through the power of the dominion anointing.

Granville Oral Roberts was born in Oklahoma in 1918; he became one of the most well-known preachers in the United States. At age seventeen he was dying of tuberculosis when his older brother took him to a tent meeting, where he was healed. Roberts later reported that on the way to the meeting, God spoke to him and said, "Son, I'm going to heal you, and you're to take my healing power to your generation."[9]

Evangelism soon became the focus of Roberts' ministry; his big-tent meetings brought an atmosphere of anticipation as his ministry blazed across America, eventually reaching around the world. He held more than three hundred crusades and personally laid hands on more than two million people. Miracles began to occur, but so did challenges. His activity as a "faith healer" brought controversy, although Roberts firmly declared, "I am not a healer. Only God can heal."[10]

Roberts was an early supporter of civil rights and insisted on the full racial integration of his audiences. To expand his outreach, he began radio broadcasts early in his ministry, following with television broadcasts, where he became a pioneer of tel-evangelism. Roberts also authored a number of books, embracing pocket-sized books to make it easier to review the lessons throughout the day. Oral Roberts' motto, "Something *good* is going to happen to you,"[11] and his revelatory teaching on "seed faith," opened the hearts of millions to the scriptural truth that

"God is a *good* God!" and that He wants to abundantly bless His people.

To advance the mission of taking the gospel into "every man's world," Oral Roberts University was built in Tulsa, Oklahoma, opening its doors in 1963. A team has been stationed at its Prayer Tower day and night for more than a half century, taking requests and offering these petitions to God. This fully accredited university has equipped thousands of men and women to take the gospel to every man's world.

Roberts remained active in ministry until his retirement in 1993 at age seventy-five, after which he and his "darling wife, Evelyn"[12] moved to California. He died in 2009 at age ninety-one, but his legacy lives on in his books, videos of his teachings and meetings, and the university that bears his name. The Oral Roberts Evangelistic Association continues in his ministry, sending teams, books, and teaching in person and online into the twenty-first century and beyond.

Rex Humbard

Ministry always begins on your knees. This is the legacy of faith Alpha Rex Emmanuel Humbard learned as the son of a rural evangelist in Arkansas. He was known as a man of deep faith, committed to prayer and soul winning throughout his life. The dominion anointing led him through seventy-five years of active ministry around the world and over the airwaves of radio and television, making a mark on every continent.

Rex Humbard followed God's leading into a life of ministry at the tender age of thirteen. In 1952 he became a pioneer in the field of televangelism from his church, Calvary Temple (later renamed the Cathedral of Tomorrow when it moved to a new facility in Cuyahoga Falls, Ohio), the first to use this new medium for the gospel. His weekly broadcast went to some sixteen hundred stations, continuing on air for more than thirty years.[13] The popular

Cathedral Quartet and Humbard's family were often seen on the program.

Humbard's broadcasts were seen in Canada, Europe, Australia, Latin American, the Middle East, the Far East, and Africa, with twenty million viewers.[14] As a result, his meetings attracted large crowds at stadiums and arenas worldwide. In 1999 *U.S. News & World Report* named Humbard one of the "Top 25 Principal Architects of the American Century."[15] He died in Florida in 2007, but the Humbard family remains committed to the work of soul winning as long as there are "people who don't know the Lord."[16] As the dominion anointing flows through his words, the ministry of Rex Humbard continues to change lives today. The dominion anointing on Rex Humbard in the rising medium of Christian television broadcasting changed the world forever.

There is no mistake that the dominion anointing has been present throughout the ages. It is still available to the chosen believer, and there are men and women who carry this precious burden today. Even the nation of Israel carries the dominion anointing. The next chapter will open the door to the release of the dominion anointing.

Chapter 26

THE DOMINION ANOINTING IN THE END TIMES

ANY BELIEVER WHO is paying attention to unfolding events knows history's clock is winding down. Those who follow biblical prophecy and those who have their thumb on the pulse of God's timetable know we are quickly approaching a very significant time in the history of the world. The dominion anointing brings these end times into focus.

Jesus talked to His disciples about two particular events that would herald the approach of the end times. We will call these two events "triggers" for the end times. We find the first one in Matthew 24:32–33 and the second one in Luke 21:24.

> Now learn a parable of the fig tree; when his branch is yet tender, and putteth forth leaves, ye know that summer is nigh: so likewise ye, when ye shall see all these things, know that it is near, even at the doors.
>
> —MATTHEW 24:32–33

The fig tree Jesus mentioned is a symbol of the nation of Israel. When Jesus says that the fig tree is tender and putting forth leaves, this tells us that these events occur when the nation of Israel is young. Hosea 9:10 says, "I found Israel like grapes in the wilderness; I saw your fathers as the firstripe [the firstfruit] in the fig tree." Every time we see the fig tree mentioned in Scripture, it is Israel. Joel 2:22 says, "Be not afraid, ye beasts of the field: for the pastures of the wilderness do spring, for the tree beareth her fruit, the fig tree and the vine do yield their strength." The vine is the church. Joel is talking about a coming revival where both the church and Israel will be blessed. I believe we are drawing closer to that time.

Understanding this, we can now see that the first trigger was 1948 when, after many centuries without a homeland for the Jewish people, Israel was recognized as a nation by the United Nations. The Lord Jesus gave this prophetic word long before it happened. I'll explain more about that as we go forward. Let's look at the second trigger.

> And they shall fall by the edge of the sword, and shall be led away captive into all nations: and Jerusalem shall be trodden down of the Gentiles, until the times of the Gentiles be fulfilled.
>
> —LUKE 21:24

The second trigger, according to Luke 21:24, occurs in Jerusalem. This verse shows that the seat of biblical Israel, the city where David set his throne, would be taken out of the hands of Israel and given over to the Gentiles for a set period of time. These events are the two biblical triggers for the end times.

I don't have room to quote all of what Jesus said about this, so I'll summarize. In Matthew 24 the Lord goes out of the temple, and they show Him the temple buildings. Jesus said, "Do you see all these things? I say to you, there won't be one stone left upon another." He meant the temple structure, not the surrounding walls.

This happened in AD 70, when Israel rebelled against Roman

rule, and the Roman Empire came down on the province with a vengeance. The temple was destroyed, and the city fell into the hands of Gentiles who took the people of Israel captive, sending them into other lands.

The study of the end times is a multifaceted, exciting subject, and people have been trying to unravel its mysteries for centuries. As Jesus sat on the Mount of Olives, the disciples asked Him for signs. "Lord, what is the sign that will tell us of Your coming? What is the *one sign* for the end of the world?" The Lord gave them a list of signs that have been going on for a long time until we get to verse 14. In verse 14 the Lord points to something quite powerful that we often miss: "And this gospel of the kingdom shall be preached in all the world for a witness unto all nations; and then shall the end come."

Preaching the gospel across all nations could not have happened in biblical times; they did not have the technology to do it. This only began to be a possibility with the dawn of the computer age and the internet, and we haven't seen the fullness of it yet. But the day will soon come when it will be possible. Jesus did not say the gospel will be preached and believed. He said "all nations" will hear the gospel as a witness.

Next, the Lord Jesus begins to break down for us what will happen. In verse 21 He says there will be great tribulation, the likes of which has never happened before. We know that is still to come in the future. Then the days will be shortened; otherwise, no flesh will survive. That is still in the future.

Now, in verse 24, as a result of this, the Antichrist—the enemy of Christ Jesus and His church—arrives on the scene. This is when the great tribulation begins. In verses 30–31 the Lord Jesus talks about His own coming. Then verse 32 says, "Now learn a parable of the fig tree; when his branch is yet tender, and putteth forth leaves, ye know that summer is nigh."

Now I will give you a little history that will explain things. In Matthew 24:34 Jesus said, "Verily I say unto you, This generation shall not pass, till all these things be fulfilled." The Lord didn't say all these generations; He focused on only one. Jesus has been talking about generations of deceptions, famines, earthquakes, wars. Then He says, "Now learn a parable of the fig tree; when his branch is yet tender, and putteth forth leaves..."

The Jewish people have existed for thousands of years. In 1948 Israel (the fig tree) did what? It was recognized as a nation by the United Nations. That was when the State of Israel was established. Branches and leaves come on a tree that has been there for a while. They do not appear on fresh young saplings.

Jesus said that when you see that happen, it is a sign of rapid growth, a quick change to the whole tree. Then He said, "So likewise ye, when ye shall see all these things, know that it is near, even at the doors" (Matt. 24:33). So 1948 is the door; it's the beginning of the last days. We've been in them since that time.

It is important to note that He used the word *verily*. "Verily I say unto you, This generation shall not pass, till all these things be fulfilled" (v. 34). *Verily* means that what is being said is undeniably true, that this will occur without fail. To understand what the Lord Jesus meant by *this generation*, we need to look at Genesis 15. It is the only chapter in the whole Bible that gives us a clear-cut answer as to how many years are in a generation.

In Genesis 15:2 Abram asks God, "What wilt thou give me, seeing I go childless?" So God takes him out, shows him the stars, makes a covenant with him, and gives him the promise. And there is a hidden key in verses 13–16:

> Know of a surety that thy seed shall be a stranger in a land
> that is not theirs, and shall serve them; and they shall afflict
> them four hundred years; and also that nation [Egypt],
> whom they shall serve, will I judge: and afterward shall they

come out with great substance. And thou shalt go to thy fathers in peace; thou shalt be buried in a good old age. But in the fourth generation they shall come hither again.

—GENESIS 15:13–16

God just told us that four hundred years is equal to four generations. They're in the land for four hundred years, and they come back in the fourth generation, clearly telling us that according to God's standard, *a generation is one hundred years*.

Armed with this understanding, we can do some simple math. If 1948 was the beginning, then adding one hundred years means the end of this generation will be 2048. No man knows the day or the hour when the Lord Jesus will return. We can, however, know the season. How much time does that give you from when you are reading this book? What will life be like in a year or two? They say that every six months the knowledge of the world is doubling. Today the world is changing quickly. Technology is rapidly altering the way we live—and increasing the chances of disease with it, by the way. But that's a topic for another time.

Let's look at something else the Lord Jesus is showing us in the Scripture. The second trigger is in Luke 21:8–24. Luke records many of the same things recorded by Matthew, but Luke is getting a whole different side of the conversation. Luke may have been an eyewitness to this, but more likely he gathered this information from others as the Holy Spirit guided him. In this way the Holy Spirit gave us Luke's Gospel to provide a broader picture of the conversation.

In Luke 21, verses 8–11 essentially repeat what was said in Matthew 24. And in Luke 21:12 the Lord Jesus identifies that this prophecy is not for our day; it was for *their* day.

> But before all these, they shall lay their hands on you, and persecute you, delivering you up to the synagogues, and

> into prisons, being brought before kings and rulers for my
> name's sake.
>
> —LUKE 21:12

That is not happening now, is it? It happened *then*. It has already taken place. It is true that today there are persecuted Christians in prisons, but the Lord is talking about people being delivered to the synagogues. Nobody goes to a synagogue to be punished today, but they did then.

Now He touches on something powerful in Luke 21:20.

> And when ye shall see Jerusalem compassed with armies,
> then know that the desolation thereof is nigh.

When did that happen? It happened in AD 70, so He's still giving us the timing of this prophecy. This prophecy is not for our day because Jerusalem has not been surrounded by any armies that we know of for two thousand years.

> Then let them which are in Judaea flee to the mountains;
> and let them which are in the midst of it depart out; and let
> not them that are in the countries enter thereinto. For these
> be the days of vengeance, that all things which are written
> may be fulfilled. But woe unto them that are with child,
> and to them that give suck, in those days! For there shall be
> great distress in the land, and wrath upon this people.
>
> —LUKE 21:21–23

Notice He talks about the land of Israel, the people of Israel. He is not talking about a worldwide tribulation time. He is talking about a time in the land and the people of Israel. We know He means the Jewish people.

Verse 24 says, "They shall fall by the edge of the sword." They did. Thousands of them were killed by the Romans in AD 132.

"And [they] shall be led away captive into all nations." They were. What year? The Romans expelled them in AD 135. Bar-Kokhba had his battle against the Romans in AD 132, and three years later the Jews were expelled from Jerusalem by the Romans. Not only were the Jews expelled, but they were also forbidden access, accurately fulfilling this verse.

Verse 24 continues, "And Jerusalem shall be trodden down of the Gentiles, until the times of the Gentiles be fulfilled." When did that happen? June 1967. That second part of the verse was fulfilled in 1967.

Two prophecies were fulfilled with precise accuracy. First, verse 20 says Jerusalem will be surrounded by armies. So it was in AD 70 when the Romans destroyed the temple. Then later, after the revolt was defeated in AD 135, the Jewish people were completely driven out of the land, fulfilling verse 24. Then, from AD 135 until 1967, the city of Jerusalem did not belong to the Jews.

I was fourteen years old in 1967 when the Six-Day War took place. I remember my dad, who was not a religious man at all at that time, walking into the house, looking at our family, and saying, "Now Jesus will come back." I'll never forget that night as long as I live. My father never mentioned Jesus in that way that I remember, except that night when the announcement was made on the radio that Jerusalem was now in the hands of the Jewish people for the first time in two thousand years. We were stunned.

The second half of verse 24 talks about another change. The Lord Jesus says, "And Jerusalem shall be trodden down of the Gentiles, until the times of the Gentiles be fulfilled," and they were. Then verse 25 says, "There shall be signs in the sun, and in the moon, and in the stars; and upon the earth distress of nations, with perplexity; the sea and the waves roaring." We have not seen verse 25 come to pass yet. We are just starting to see the very edges of the beginning of it.

Verses 26 and 27 tell us,

> Men's hearts failing them for fear, and for looking after
> those things which are coming on the earth: for the powers
> of heaven shall be shaken. And then shall they see the Son
> of man coming in a cloud with power and great glory.

Here the Lord Jesus gave us a fantastic key: Jerusalem. Now there is a battle today over what? Jerusalem. The world is screaming that Jerusalem needs to be divided. Well, I have news for them: the Lord Jesus is not coming back to a divided Jerusalem.

In the news today we hear talk about dividing the city. It will never happen. They can talk about it all they want. It will not happen. Ariel Sharon made a decision after peace with Egypt when they gave away Sinai. He said, now let's not give away Jerusalem too, so they began building settlements all around it. To give away Jerusalem would cause a civil war in Israel because you now have cities all around the city. You cannot change that. You cannot remove hundreds of thousands of Jewish people living in those settlements. It would cause an uprising the likes of which has never been seen in two thousand years. There would be bloodshed like we have never seen in Israel, so it will not happen. Jerusalem will never be divided, no matter how much they believe it and no matter how much the world wants it.

The Old Testament prophet Zechariah says that the last war will occur because of Jerusalem, and millions of Israel's enemies will die. Let me give you a little history before I continue because it will be very intriguing for you. Here's the exciting thing that you need to know about 1948 and 1967: In 1948, it's reported, the great British general Bernard Montgomery said, "I give them two weeks before they're wiped off the map," because there were six hundred thousand against forty million. Israel had one cannon—*one cannon*—against five armies with more weaponry, tanks, and planes than you could imagine. Guess how many planes Israel had? One. How many bombs were in the plane? Zero! What did they throw out of the plane? Soda bottles.

You read that right. To win a battle against Egyptian tanks, they used soda bottles. The tanks came close to the city of Tel Aviv, and there was no way to stop them. So the Israelis took one plane up in the air and threw soda bottles, which made a whistling sound as they fell through the air. The Egyptian tanks thought they were bombs, and they fled. So God won the battle with soda bottles!

In the natural it looked impossible, but Israel is still here! God performed a miracle in 1948, and Israel stunned the world by winning a war and becoming a nation. Do you want to know where the dominion anointing is today? *The dominion anointing resides in the nation of Israel.*

Having said all this about 1948, I want to say a little more about 1967. In 1967 what would be known as the Six-Day War started with a Soviet lie. The Russians wanted to prove that their weapons were better than American weapons, and because of the Vietnam War, America was having difficulties. So the Soviets decided to lie to the Syrians and say that Israel was going to attack them. That's how the war began.

At that time, President Nasser of Egypt had an agreement with the Syrians that if Israel attacked Syria, he would defend Syria. The Russians convinced him that the Israelis were going to attack Syria, and that is when Nasser got on the radio and began to beat the drums of war. By the time he found out the report was not accurate, it was too late to stop the riots on the streets. That is how the war began.

The result was a fulfillment of prophecy. God's prophecy was fulfilled by the Soviets' lie. Think about that. "Surely the wrath of man shall praise thee" (Ps. 76:10). It is incredible how God uses what happens on earth to fulfill His Word.

The year 1967 was a trigger year. After that men went to the moon and we saw an explosion in technology. The first trigger in 1948 brought changes worldwide that still affect our lives, and 1967 brought more advances that affect our lives even to this day, including technology, communication, and medicine. Now we are facing some frightening events.

Things Yet to Come

What will happen first is extreme weather. You may or may not believe in climate change, but Isaiah 24:5–6 says this:

> The earth also is defiled under the inhabitants thereof; because they have transgressed the laws, changed the ordinance, broken the everlasting covenant. Therefore hath the curse devoured the earth, and they that dwell therein are desolate: therefore the inhabitants of the earth are burned.

The Bible tells us very clearly about the judgments coming. Hailstones will fall on the earth that weigh one hundred pounds each. Whether you believe in climate change doesn't matter. What matters is what the Bible says about the coming days. In recent years Australia has had its hottest temperatures ever, temperatures that reached 121 degrees Fahrenheit. Phenomena like this will happen worldwide. I am not saying this because some scientists told me; I am saying it because I read it in the Bible.

> And the fourth angel poured out his vial upon the sun; and power was given unto him to scorch men with fire. And men were scorched with great heat, and blasphemed the name of God, which hath power over these plagues: and

they repented not....And there fell upon men a great hail out of heaven, every stone about the weight of a talent.

—Revelation 16:8–9, 21

That is the weather change I'm talking about: the sun and heat scorching people and hailstones that weigh a talent, which is one hundred pounds. And men do what? Blaspheme God because of the plague of the hail. There is fire scorching them in one place and hail killing them in another. Well, that's climate change too.

I go by the Word of God, and it says that extreme changes in the weather are coming. And no matter what the governments around the world agree to do to slow or stop it, the changes will come. Legislation and agreements made by men cannot prevent the Word of God from taking place just as He said it would.

Let's look at something else that's already happening. Malaysia has been implementing a cashless society. They no longer use cash in Malaysia. Not only that, but today, worldwide, how many people go into a bank anymore? We're using computers, debit cards, and apps on phones to pay bills. We're now beginning to go into electronic cash and Bitcoin. Here is the definition of Bitcoin: "trademark in the UK, a type of digital currency in which a record of transactions is maintained in new units of currency which are generated by the computational solution of mathematical problems and which operates independently of Central Bank."

This is already happening. A few years ago I was in South Africa, walking in the mall, and I saw machines everywhere. I asked someone what all the machines were for, and they told me, "Digital cash." I said, "What?" I began looking it up, and I was stunned that these things were happening and I did not even know about it. We are coming into a cashless society very quickly worldwide. And what does this say to me? It says that the mark of the beast is almost here.

We've got Bitcoin, and now they're eliminating passports in

Australia. All airports in Australia have facial recognition. So your face now is your passport in Australia, and it's coming to the world. Everywhere around the world they're moving away from paper. Facial recognition is now taking over in some parts of the world. In fact, in the United States they're talking about eliminating the TSA. In light of the COVID shutdown, they're talking about eliminating TSA and going into facial recognition in airports.

Let's look at what Jesus says in Luke 18:1–8.

> And he spake a parable unto them to this end, that men ought always to pray, and not to faint; saying, There was in a city a judge, which feared not God, neither regarded man: and there was a widow in that city; and she came unto him, saying, Avenge me of mine adversary. And he would not for a while: but afterward he said within himself, Though I fear not God, nor regard man; yet because this widow troubleth me, I will avenge her, lest by her continual coming she weary me. And the Lord said, Hear what the unjust judge saith. And shall not God avenge his own elect, which cry day and night unto him, though he bear long with them?... Nevertheless when the Son of man cometh, shall he find faith on the earth?

I've always been amazed by the Lord's statement "Will I find faith on the earth?" Now, I look at this portion of Scripture, and then I begin to read about artificial intelligence (AI), essentially where computers are learning for themselves and solving problems humans can't solve. I've also been learning about cyborg technology. If you aren't familiar with it, cyborg technology, in a nutshell, is the meshing of biology and technology, upgrading our old human hardware with electronic hardware. It's upgraded limbs, upgraded eyes, and eventually upgraded organs. An expert has said that beyond biometric limbs, they now have something called a "digital tattoo," which is essentially a microchip that can be inlaid under the skin. He said it would be like putting an Apple watch underneath the skin, a subdermal Apple watch.

When will this happen? The technology, for the most part, is available as I write this. It is a matter of when it will be implemented on a wide scale. The technology to do it already exists. So the system of the Antichrist is already here, waiting to be unleashed.

We are hearing about AI taking over dangerous jobs because they don't want to see people harmed with dangerous work. It is already happening; machines are doing it. People are talking about solving climate change with AI. The machines can do studies we humans cannot; the experts say that AI will figure out climate change for humanity to prevent catastrophic weather events from coming. Think about the enormous amount of data available for worldwide weather activities, and being able to process that data, and then being able to predict that data based on the past.

Things are changing fast. As soon as this book is printed, some of the things I've written here will be outdated. New technology emerges every day. But my point is that we are closer than we think when it comes to the system of the Antichrist.

The Bible tells us to look for two things in 2 Thessalonians 2:3:

1. A great falling away

2. The "man of sin" (Antichrist) being revealed

The falling away will be before this system of the Antichrist is in total control. If we look around, it isn't difficult to see that the falling away has begun with what is going on in churches today. The gospel is not being preached as it once was. We no longer hear about the cross, about the blood, about sanctification, about repentance. There is a lot of universalism out there and a lot of preaching that everyone will go to heaven. Any belief system outside of biblical precedents is untrue. Scripture is our standard. We are now at a stage where we have to again contend for the faith, as Jude said in his day when they were denying that the Lord Jesus is the Son of God.

(In our current day we are having to deal with clever deceptions being touted as truth everywhere. I hear it more and more, and it is troubling to me.)Some people say that God is too loving to send people to hell, so everyone's going to heaven. Everyone is saved, but they don't know it. But I have to go back to the Bible. We have to think about our destiny in Jesus. What will He tell us when we stand before the judgment seat?

2045

Chapter 27

THE KEYS TO SEALING
YOUR VICTORY

PRAYER. PRAYER IS the master key that unlocks the door to a victorious life and a powerfully effective ministry. These are perilous times, but we are not helpless or hopeless. *We have prayer.* Where there are praying believers, there is a listening God, ready to intervene and equip us with everything required for this walk of faith. In Luke 21:36 Jesus points to prayer as the key to escaping the difficult days that are unfolding before our very eyes:

> Watch ye therefore, and pray always, that ye may be accounted worthy to escape all these things that shall come to pass, and to stand before the Son of man.

TEN KEYS TO SURVIVAL IN THE LORD'S PRAYER

The key to survival is prayer. The Lord's Prayer contains a full set of keys and is the perfect pattern for prayer that Jesus gave us. When they came to the Lord in Luke 11 and Matthew 6 and said, "Teach us to pray," Jesus gave the most powerful keys for survival in Scripture's most famous prayer.

Key 1

The Lord Jesus began by saying, "Our Father" (Matt. 6:9). You cannot have a powerful life of prayer without a relationship with God. When the Lord began with the words, "Our Father," He was talking about something significant and powerful. Only by the Holy Spirit are we able to have this personal relationship with the Father. In Romans 8:15 and Galatians 4:6, it is the Spirit who says Abba Father. Relationship is key. The first thing we must develop is a relationship with God the Father.

And today, many believers lack that understanding of relationship. Do we know God the Father? Many people talk about God the Son and God the Holy Spirit, but the Lord Jesus made it very clear: we must have a relationship with the Father. And that happens through Jesus. God will not hear those who have no relationship with Him. We must develop our relationship with the Father.

Key 2

Jesus said, "Which art in heaven" (v. 9). That means our citizenship; we have to recognize that we are citizens of heaven. We must pray from the perspective that our citizenship is in glory. We know from Scripture that we are citizens of heaven.

> But our citizenship is in heaven. And we eagerly await a Savior from there, the Lord Jesus Christ.
> —PHILIPPIANS 3:20, NIV

In the first minute of our salvation we become citizens of heaven, and we have rights. If you are an American, you have rights today as a citizen of the United States. We have *greater* rights as citizens of heaven. To establish yourself as a citizen of heaven, you must disconnect from the earth. Look to heaven. "Set your affection on things above," Paul said in Colossians 3:2.

When you set your affections on things above, you become disconnected from the earth. It is impossible to disconnect from the earth if you keep looking at it and what it represents. I have no interest in anything the world has to offer because that connects you to the earth.

When I see people connected to earthly things, I know they have not embraced their heavenly citizenship. God wants us to be true citizens of heaven, and citizens of heaven are involved with heaven, not earth. We are *in* the world, not *of* it, plain and simple.

> Now therefore ye are no more strangers and foreigners, but
> fellow citizens with the saints, and of the household of God.
> —EPHESIANS 2:19

You might say, "How do I disconnect from the earth?" Stop watching things that are beneath your heavenly citizenship. Stop being involved in the affairs of this life. It's quite simple. Everyone knows how to disconnect. Just shut it out. Shut the world out.

Key 3

You must build your worship. "Hallowed be thy name" (v. 9). That is adoration. It means entering into the realm of worship. Not only are we to develop our relationship and citizenship, but we are also to develop our worship.

Key 4

Jesus said, "Thy kingdom come" (v. 10). That means I put His interests ahead of mine. "Thy kingdom come" has to do with the destruction of the kingdom of evil in my life. It means I am to have no connection whatsoever to the satanic, no relationship with the flesh. I am responsible for shutting it out of my life. His kingdom coming *into my life* is what the Lord meant when He said, "Thy kingdom come." How does His kingdom come into my life? By dismissing all other kingdoms out of my life. I don't allow demonic influences or worldly connections. I shut the door and walk away from anything that would hinder the kingdom of God in my life.

There are Christians watching filth, and they think nothing is wrong with it. That's a doorway to the demonic. Slam that door shut! How can the kingdom of God be in them if they're watching evil things and taking it into their eyes, which are the windows of their souls? I am not saying you can only watch biblical films, but please do not watch worldly or demonic movies or read material in books or magazines that give place to ungodliness in your life. You have to make a covenant with your eyes to say, "I will not watch this. I will not read this. I just will not do it." Shut it out. I know that is getting tougher to do because of the internet, but ultimately, it is your choice. *It is your responsibility.*

Key 5

Jesus said, "Thy will be done" (v. 10). This means we have to know His Word. You cannot know His will without knowing His Word. It is absolutely impossible. When the Lord said, "Thy will be done," He was saying, "It is time for you to know His mind. It is time for you to know His revealed will, which is the Bible." After you know His mind, His will, then you can confidently make your petition known.

Key 6

Jesus said, "Give us this day our daily bread" (v. 11). I cannot pray effectively unless (1) I know Him, (2) I know my citizenship, (3) I know worship, (4) I'm living in the kingdom, and (5) I know His mind, His will. Then and only then are my petitions, my requests heard because the next thing Jesus said is, "Give us this day our daily bread." This tells me that once I have right relationship, right citizenship, right worship, and His kingdom and His Word in my life, I can bring my petitions.

Philippians 4:6 says that God wants to know the details of your needs. The Scripture says, "Be careful for nothing; but in every thing by prayer and supplication with thanksgiving let your requests be made known unto God." Now when Paul said "everything," he meant tell God the details in your petitions.

Most people begin making petitions before they even know who they're talking to. That's the problem. We have to develop what I've just been writing about. And the Lord Jesus put it perfectly in order. He said you couldn't make petitions until everything was in place. Then you make your petitions known to Him.

Key 7

After you bring your petitions, which God will hear, Jesus said, "Forgive us our debts" (v. 12). Just what does that mean? This is actually quite powerful. It is the only thing that brings answers to the petitions. You make your requests, and then you forgive to receive answers to your requests. Without forgiveness, you can forget about getting the answer. You can pray all you want, but if you are not doing what the Lord said to do, it will not work.

Key 8

Jesus said, "Lead us not into temptation" (v. 13). After forgiveness comes deliverance, meaning we don't do it again. We don't confess and then keep confessing because we are not free yet. True deliverance follows all the other things in Jesus' prayer. How can you be delivered if you do not know God, know your citizenship, develop your worship, and commit to the principles I just showed you? Without total obedience, there is no way to be delivered. You are still living in an old kingdom until you decide you are ready to completely obey God.

Key 9

Jesus said, "Deliver us from evil," or the evil one (v. 13). That is a prayer of strength, and that is when we receive deliverance from the schemes of the devil. That is when we are able to resist the devil.

> Submit yourselves therefore to God. Resist the devil, and he
> will flee from you.
>
> —JAMES 4:7

Key 10

Jesus prayed, "For thine is the kingdom, and the power, and the glory" (v. 13). In this way, He seals the prayer again with praise. Praise finishes our process. We thank Him, we praise Him, we bless His name for hearing us.

These ten strategic keys keep you safe and they secure your longevity. So I bring this teaching on mysteries of the anointing to a close because I just gave you the keys that will help you to be victorious in this life. You have all that you need, and if you use what you have learned, you can overcome by the power of Christ and His anointing in you, even during these perilous times.

MYSTERIES OF THE ANOINTING REVEALED

Mysteries of the anointing are now revealed, truths that will launch you into glorious new heights. You cannot build much without tools. You now have tools to build a purposeful and powerful life and a mighty ministry that are marked by God's anointing. It's the anointing that makes the difference.

I desire for your heart to be encouraged to cultivate a

meaningful and intimate daily walk with the Lord. This is of paramount importance and foundational in the message of this teaching. You now possess the keys to unlocking the limitless potential that God has placed within you.

As we draw to the close of this book, we can see that the subject of mysteries of the anointing is both broad and deep. When you first saw this title, I believe that your interest was aroused because you have a sincere desire for a greater manifestation of God's anointing in and on your life.

I trust that as these pages have shone a light on God's anointing, your understanding of this power from on high has been ignited. I pray that you will take what you have learned here, apply it, and continue to move forward into a deeper measure of His presence and His power that is pure and personal, walking in an unbroken flow of His precious anointing.

> Now unto him that is able to keep you from falling, and to present you faultless before the presence of his glory with exceeding joy, to the only wise God our Saviour, be glory and majesty, dominion and power, both now and ever. Amen.
>
> —JUDE 24–25

Even so, come, Lord Jesus.

—REVELATION 22:20

NOTES

CHAPTER 1

1. C. H. Spurgeon, *The Treasury of David: Containing an Original Exposition of the Book of Psalms; a Collection of Illustrative Extracts From the Whole Range of Literature; a Series of Homiletical Hints Upon Almost Every Verse; and Lists of Writers Upon Each Psalm*, vol. 1 (London: Robert Culley, 1870), 402.

CHAPTER 9

1. "Intro: Prayer," Life Church Bradford, January 6, 2019, https://www.lifechurchbradford.com/intro-to-prayer/.

CHAPTER 25

1. "The Goose" (Jan Hus), Lutheran Press, accessed January 4, 2022, https://lutheranpress.com/the-swan/.
2. "I Felt My Heart Strangely Warmed," Journal of John Wesley, accessed January 4, 2022, https://www.ccel.org/ccel/wesley/journal.vi.ii.xvi.html.
3. John Wesley, "Free Grace. A Sermon Preached at Bristol," Evans Early American Imprint Collection, accessed January 4, 2022, https://quod.lib.umich.edu/e/evans/N03929.0001.001/1:4?rgn=div1;view=fulltext.
4. Joe Iovino, "God Is With Us: Blessing the Dying and Those Who Grieve," UMC.org, accessed January 4, 2022, http://ee.umc.org/what-we-believe/god-is-with-us-blessing-the-dying-and-those-who-grieve.

5. Randall Herbert Balmer, *Encyclopedia of Evangelicalism* (Waco, TX: Baylor University Press, 2004), 128.

6. Albert B. Simpson, "A Missionary Cry," Hymnary.org, accessed January 4, 2022, https://hymnary.org/text/a_hundred_thousand_souls_a_day.

7. Charlotte Elliott, "Just as I Am, Without One Plea," Hymnary.org, 1790, https://hymnary.org/text/just_as_i_am_without_one_plea.

8. Billy Graham, "What's 'the Billy Graham Rule'?," Billy Graham Evangelistic Association, July 23, 2019, https://billygraham.org/story/the-modesto-manifesto-a-declaration-of-biblical-integrity/.

9. Richard Roberts, *He's a Healing Jesus* (Tulsa, OK: Oral Roberts Evangelistic Association, 2013).

10. Ernie Keen, "'Only God Can Heal' Oral Roberts Tells Souls Crusade Audience Here," *Tulsa World*, February 22, 2019, https://tulsaworld.com/archive/only-god-can-heal-oral-roberts-tells-souls-crusade-audience-here/article_249d4428-8edc-523c-a73e-afe23f8bb54a.html.

11. Also the title of a book by Richard Roberts, about his father (Tulsa, OK: Albury Publishing, 1996).

12. Evelyn Roberts, *His Darling Wife, Evelyn: The Autobiography of Mrs. Oral Roberts* (New York: Dial Press, 1976).

13. "Alpha Rex Emmanuel Humbard (1919–2007)," Encyclopedia of Arkansas, accessed January 4, 2022, https://encyclopediaofarkansas.net/entries/alpha-rex-emmanuel-humbard-4530/.

14. Michael Pollak, "Rex Humbard, TV Evangelist, Dies at 88," *New York Times*, September 23, 2007, https://www.nytimes.com/2007/09/23/us/23humbard.html.

15. "Alpha Rex Emmanuel Humbard," TVDays, accessed January 4, 2022, https://www.tvdays.com/rex-humbard.

16. "Faith & Support," Rex Humbard Foundation, accessed January 4, 2022, https://rexhumbard.org/faith-support/.

Prayers if only 1 - 4 peoples

1 - 1,000. to flight
2 - 10,000 " "
3 - 100,000 " "
4 - 1,000,000 "